The Revived Church

Church

*A Challenge for
Tomorrow's Church Today*

Roger Helland

Sovereign World

Sovereign World Ltd
PO Box 777
Tonbridge
Kent TN11 0ZS

ISBN: 1 85240 232 6

This Sovereign World book is distributed in North America by Renew
Books, a ministry of Gospel Light, Ventura, California, USA. For a free
catalog of resources from Renew Books/Gospel Light, please contact your
Christian supplier or call 1–800–4–GOSPEL.

Typeset by CRB Associates, Reepham, Norfolk.
Printed in the UK by Clays Ltd, St Ives plc

Acknowledgements

Thanks to my loyal wife Gail and my wonderful children Melissa, Joel and Micah. You all endured yet another book with me. I love you more than words can express. Thanks for your patience with me, especially those times when I tied up your use of the computer and was holed up by myself when I could have been with you.

Thanks to Wesley and Stacey Campbell for giving me some crucial last minute input, for promoting this book, and for giving me the helm of a fantastic church. As you help foster revived churches, to use your words, 'Just don't die!'

Thanks to Gord and Jan Whyte for always pushing for more of the Spirit and helping our people get healed and whole. We've been together a long time! May Isaiah 61 be your portion.

Thanks to Ralph and Donna Bromley for your ability to unscramble scrambled eggs along with your commitment to intercession, discipleship, mercy, and kingdom world-views.

Thanks to Richard and Sherryl Anderton for giving us nine years of your life at New Life and for five of those years influencing the children for God. May God bless your church plant.

Thanks to Nathan and Kendra Rieger for joining our team. What a magnificent asset you are and Nathan for being the consummate 'passionary' for Jesus and justice!

Thanks to Malcolm and Donna Petch for being examples of humility, servanthood, and perseverance. Thanks for 'wrestling with worship' for so long with us!

Thanks to Jim and Marie Rolfe for your 'ministry of wandering around' and loving our people. You will have a bag of rewards in heaven that will be too heavy to lift.

Thanks to Shawn and Reece Worsfold for letting us meet in your home so much and for your constant enthusiasm, persistence and love for our people and the ministry of Jesus.

Thanks to Gerald, Darlene, Rita, and Carol for being those pillar saints that work behind the scenes to keep up with the rest of us. I notice your unwavering loyalty and hard work.

Thanks to James Ryle who always empowers me with the Word and the Spirit and 'incites' me with 'insight.' I have personally embraced your four-word description of 'freedom.'

Thanks to Matt and Laura Atkins for your steadfast friendship and your inquiring hearts for effective leadership and ministry. I love you and your five great children immensely.

Thanks to Chris Mungeam for responding to a 'leading' of the Holy Spirit to contact me about getting this book into print this year and for praying for my ailing mother-in-law who was critically ill in hospital at the time. She has recovered because of prayer. You are a revived publisher! Thanks also to Tim Pettingale who was always swift to answer my e-mails.

Thanks to Len Hjalmarson and Allan Love who analyzed the entire manuscript and offered valuable comments and suggestions. You both have sharp understanding of the way of the heart.

Finally, thanks to the people of New Life Vineyard Fellowship for being such an awesome church. I dearly love you all.

About the Author

Roger Helland serves as Senior Pastor, and was a member of the founding team, of New Life Vineyard Fellowship in Kelowna, B.C. Canada. Roger is a graduate of Dallas Theological Seminary, former Bible College instructor, and author of *Let the River Flow: Welcoming Renewal Into Your Church*. He teaches on church renewal, leadership, biblical interpretation and the gifts and ministries of the Holy Spirit. As a Bible teacher he has ministered in a variety of inter-denominational settings in various parts of the world. His vision is to balance the Word and the Spirit and see people equipped, empowered and released to fulfill their vision to serve Jesus Christ. Roger lives in Kelowna with his wife Gail and their three children.

For conference ministry, teaching tapes or books contact:

Roger Helland
Freedom Ministries
505 Brighton Road
Kelowna, British Columbia
Canada
V1X 5K6

E-mail: rhelland@wkpowerlink.com
Fax: 250–765–1323 or 250–861–3844
Website: www.newlife.bc.ca

If you enjoy this book and would like to help us to send a
copy of it and many other titles to needy pastors in the
Third World, please write for further information
or send your gift to:

**Sovereign World Trust
PO Box 777, Tonbridge
Kent TN11 0ZS
United Kingdom**

or to the **'Sovereign World'** distributor in your country.

Contents

Foreword

The *Revived Church* is not another church growth book, which begins and ends with the human factors of program and commitment. It is a book about dependence on the Spirit of God for developing a revived church. If you are under the impression that a church moved upon by the Spirit of God is thus free of problems you have obviously never been part of one. This book faces the move of God in the church today realistically and without denial. Yet, it faces squarely the conditions that always come with such a move.

It is a book about vision and leadership in the vortex of Holy Spirit revival, about learning to pastor the power of God beyond the level of blessings sought and found. It carries the caution of violating the delicate balance between the necessity of the power of the Holy Spirit and correctness of biblical doctrine with proper application and methods.

It is a book about the river and the banks of the river in which it is contained and directed. These both are necessities if the flow of God's Spirit is to be sustained in the church. It is not enough to have the surge of the spiritual floods. The floods must be held in coherence for direction and intensity. Otherwise, the result of the surge will be a temporary phenomenon with great, possible dangers and little or no lasting effect.

It is a book about joy and how church-going ought to be. The joy of relating, the joy of worshipping, the joy of balancing excitement with direction, and yes, the joy of continuing repentance. It is a much-needed work about how to behave and believe in the midst of a move of the Spirit with a call to be mindful of the pitfalls and potential problems which always accompany a move of God. It is a map often needed in times of rapid and sometimes violent transition when confusion abounds and tempers flare. It is a call to the primacy of prayer with more than just the worn cliché 'we ought to pray more.' The whole chapter on 'Praying With Fire' is extremely helpful and challenging.

In these days, which present a danger the church has seldom had to manage, this work sounds out solid instruction on how to direct the fire without quenching it, how to harness the river without damming it and how to translate the power into continuing and practical dynamics without cutting off the switch altogether.

In this work, Helland again and again calls us to learn from history and not repeat its errors and to listen to the men of God who now watch from the grandstands of heaven. He allows for the **fun** which accompanies the first waves of the Spirit's coming but challenges us to go on to the **fear** of God which alone results in holiness and consecration.

Among the final conclusions is that which all of us need to remember, namely, that the movement God has initiated **is itself moving** and we must move with it onward, outward and upward. The truth which must be kept paramount while this is taking place is that those of us fortunate enough to be involved in what God is doing must be people of brokenness, continuing humility, rapid repentance and accelerated obedience.

This work deserves as wide an application as it demands a wide distribution and readership.

Jack Taylor
Dimension Ministries
Melbourne, Florida

What Others Are Saying About
The Revived Church

Roger Helland has given us one of the best books on the subject of leading a church in renewal and growth that I have ever read. The author writes from a background of scholarship, wide-reading and personal experience. This great book says so well what I truly believe, and I just wish I could have written it myself. We've needed this kind of book for years. Highly readable from end to end it is impossible to put down once started – except to copy its profound insights and choice quotes.

Bishop David Pytches
St. Andrews Church
Chorleywood, England

Don't miss reading *The Revived Church*. Every page provides lively, stirring and weighty answers to the challenge of cultivating revived churches for the new millennium. Roger demonstrates insightful and prophetic understanding coupled with real life experience. This is not a heady, academic book, it is practical and passionate, for leaders and lay-people alike, from a guy who's been there, who's doing it and who's living it!

Wesley Campbell
Revival Now!
Kelowna, British Columbia, Canada

In a time when sound judgment, biblical principles and spiritual common sense are in desperate need, Roger has met these three in a well-researched, well-documented and well-written work on developing revived churches. Well done, Roger!

Frank Damazio
Senior Pastor, Bible Temple
Portland, Oregon

Roger's book is jam-packed with vision, ideas, and examples on what it means to be a revived church in the new millennium. He demonstrates a compelling passion for the Word and the Spirit as he appeals for the renewal of the church leading to revival. Writing from first-hand experience, he treats his subject with a healthy balance of biblical and practical guidance. His understanding and heart for renewal and revival is evident throughout. I recommend it to all Christians, to both lay-people and pastors.

Mike Bickle
Senior Pastor, Metro Christian Fellowship
Kansas City, Missouri

The Revived Church is intensely practical, full of rich and little known quotes and statistics. It is passionate. This book should be read by every frustrated Christian and pastoral leader!

Gerald Coates
Pioneer People
London, England

Roger Helland is not only a well-trained theologian but is also Senior Pastor of a great and progressive church. He is well-equipped through his own personal encounter with the Holy Spirit as well as years of involvement in a local church that has been in sustained renewal and revival. His insights into building a revived church will be invaluable.

John Arnott
Senior Pastor
Toronto Airport Christian Fellowship
Toronto, Canada

The need has never been greater for the Spirit-sensitive Church to become pragmatic in pursuing realistic fulfillment of fantastic dreams and visions. I believe Roger Helland has written a book to help close the gap between dreaming and doing. I heartily recommend it for pastors and parishioners alike!

James Ryle
Senior Pastor, Vine Life Community Church
Boulder, Colorado

The Revived Church – a challenge for the most gifted of leaders. Roger weaves great insight with personal experience to give us a helpful map in navigating the always exciting, and at times treacherous waters, on the way to becoming great churches. If your compass is set towards being a revived community this book will help you stay on course!

David Ruis
Senior Pastor, Vineyard Christian Fellowship
Winnipeg Centre, Winnipeg, Canada

Here is a stimulating and practical study, brimming with useful ideas and concepts, that delivers what it promises, guiding people from the blessing of renewal into the bounty of revival. Hungry Christians will find some real meat here!

Dr Michael L. Brown
President, Brownsville Revival School of Ministry
Pensacola, Florida

Roger has a unique and perceptive ability to read the times. I am certain that this book will be a valuable tool to all building a New Testament church in this day and generation. His insight and analysis I'm sure will be a help to Christians everywhere. Most of all, the breath of the Spirit through the pages of this book encourages us all to maintain the fire in our hearts, spread it to our communities and burn brightly for the glory of the Father.

Ken Gott
Revival Now!
Sunderland, UK

The Revived Church is not only a fresh breath from mere methodology and programs, but actually, is a necessary read for the contemporary church builder. Roger manages to represent that new breed of leader that is managing to 'marry' the things of the Word and the Spirit. Without sacrificing overall perspective, he brings forth the necessity of blending the new with the old. I seriously recommend this book for all.

Marc A. Dupont
Mantle of Praise Ministries
Toronto Airport Christian Fellowship

I had a hard time putting this book down. Where else will we find a seasoned pastor combine solid biblical theology, the dynamic of the Holy Spirit, years of hands-on ministry, a wide background in leadership and the 'how to's of church ministry with a clear prophetic voice for the future? There is nothing abstract here. Principles are demonstrated by personal experience honestly hammered out in a dynamic church coming alive. Get this book. Give it to leaders and people alike. You will be challenged and your church will be changed.

Dr Don Williams
Pastor, The Coast Vineyard Christian Fellowship
La Jolla, California

Four words describe Roger Helland's book: Radical, Grounded, Inspirational, and Practical. It is filled with a rare combination of Fire and Wisdom. The message of this book needs to be heard loud and clear as the church moves into the next century.

Jim W. Goll
Ministry to the Nations
Antioch, Tennessee

I believe Roger Helland has captured the raw essence of the dilemmas that the Fire of God will bring. The understanding that can be gleaned from this book will go a long way in preparing the church and leaders for God's fire in their midst in the 21st century.

John Paul Jackson
Senior Pastor, Shiloh House Community Church
Fort Worth, Texas

Introduction

A Vision for a Revived Church for the 21st Century

As a student, I sat in a Dallas Seminary class and listened to a humorous exhortation by Professor Howard Hendricks. He stepped to the lectern, pulled his glasses from his nose, and leaned forward to make a point. 'Gentlemen, in every church there are two kinds of people – pillars and caterpillars. Pillars support the church with strength and dignity. Caterpillars just crawl in and out every Sunday and fuzz up the place.' My dear reader, are you a pillar or a caterpillar? What kind of people support revived churches? The answer is obvious. Do you feebly settle for just fuzzing up the place? Or do you want to be a more effective pillar ready to help support your church? Maybe you already do but now you want to become stronger. In either case, this book is for you.

Today we are entering probably the most massive season of revival that the world has ever seen. Bill Bright predicts global revival by the year 2000. Mike Bickle predicts that God will change the understanding and expression of Christianity in one generation. God is literally pouring out His Spirit according to Acts 2. Like one lady I talked to said, 'Roger, I am so full of God I think I'm going to blow up.' Ordinary Christians are becoming revived. They are finding joy like the Methodists during the Second Great Awakening in America (ca. 1776–1810). A humorous conversation between the Methodist circuit rider Francis Asbury and Charles, his apprentice, makes the point.

Charles approached. 'Heard you went to a Methodist meetin'.'

'Sure did.'

'Any shoutin'?'

'Some.'

'Why do Methodists shout?'

'Because they're happy.'

Charles sighed. 'Can't see how anyone could be happy in church. Whenever I go I feel like a corpse.'

'Why are you bored in church?'

'Because it's the same thing every Sunday.' [1]

At church, have you ever felt like a corpse? We all have. But because of the renewal of the 90s, thousands of Christians have discovered new joy in Jesus. They've become 'shoutin' Methodists.' For the first time in their lives, crowds of housewives, husbands, pastors and people, youth and kids, are swimming in the River of 'the Father's blessing.' But after they are blessed, what next? After renewal, where to? That's what this book is about. It's about how Christians and leaders can release renewal in ways that will empower and revive their churches. It's about how to **get** but also **go beyond** renewal and balance the Word and the Spirit.

Now, let your imagination soar. Imagine a church alive with the 'Untamed God.' A church buzzing with people absolutely sold out for God. Thick with God's presence, filled with passionate worship, where people get their tanks filled through anointed Bible preaching and teaching. A church known as a powerhouse of prayer and friendship, throbbing with joyful and loving people who generously help each other as they meet together on Sundays and throughout the week in homes. A church radiant with awe because of miraculous signs and wonders. Now, imagine throngs of people who regularly come to Christ and join that church. They get dunked in water and in the Holy Spirit. Sounds like a revived church doesn't it? Is that the kind of church you want to be a pillar in? You say, 'Man, I'd love to. Is it possible?' Well, have a look at Acts 2:41–47 and notice the words 'those,' 'they,' 'everyone,' 'all' used of ordinary Christians.

'Those who accepted his message were baptized, and about three thousand were added to their number that day. They devoted themselves to the apostles' teaching and to the fellowship, to the breaking of bread and to prayer. Everyone was filled with awe, and many wonders and miraculous signs were done by the apostles. All the believers were together and had everything in common. Selling their possessions and goods, they gave to anyone as he had need. Every day they continued to meet together in the temple courts. They broke bread in their homes and ate together with glad and sincere hearts, praising God and enjoying the favor of all the people. And the Lord added to their number daily those who were being saved.'

Maybe you resist, 'Yeah, but that was the early Church, a time of transition, of revival. I'm not sure that's a realistic model for my church today.' Well, why did Luke write the book of Acts? He wrote it to document what **normal** church life and mission looks like and to inspire his readers with vision for it. Can you catch the vision? It's hard to build without it.

Vision is a dream, a preferred future, a feeling in one's heart and a seeing in one's mind of a picture of what is possible. Vision is an expression of destination, of ideal, of optimism, of where you want to live. What is your vision for your church? Ponder Ephesians 3:20:

'Now to him who is able to do immeasurably more than all we ask or imagine, according to his power that is at work within us.'

The problem with many Christians and leaders is not how much God can do, but with how much they can imagine according to God's power living in them!

Warren G. Bennis says, 'Leadership is the capacity to translate vision into reality.' My vision is to be a church like the one in Acts 2:41–47. How about you? My vision is to also help others fulfill their visions – to translate that vision into reality. My purpose is to provide some inspiration and instruction in things that I'm learning about church ministry (first as a layman and now as a pastor). I am not **the** expert and our church is not **the** example. This book is not

the standard on what constitutes a revived church. Nevertheless, I will suggest things that might help us get from ideas to implementation.

In Part One, I'll encourage you to apply the principles of The Word: Building the Fireplace. In Part Two, I'll encourage you to apply the principles of The Spirit: Fanning the Flame. My purpose is that after you have experienced renewal, you will translate your vision into reality through the art and science of building fireplaces and fanning flames for a revived church for the 21st century. For a possible blueprint, read on.

PART ONE

The Word:
Building the Fireplace

Chapter 1

The Revived Church

*'We are sometimes so interested in creating the machinery
of the church that we let the fire go out in the boiler.'*
(Arkansas Baptist)

*'The test of a good church bulletin, like the restaurant's
menu, is whether or not the establishment can deliver what
is listed in the contents.'*
(Leonard Klotz)

I was invited to speak at a 'Send Your Rain' conference. People
from twelve denominations assembled in remarkable unity to
pursue God for renewal in their valley. The forecast was for
sunny skies but it rained all weekend. I believe the rain was
prophetic. Something else was also prophetic: the conference
was held in the newly built sanctuary of the First Christian
Reformed Church. In the front of the property were the
remains from the old sanctuary – the concrete foundation,
the stairs and piles of rotted wood. On that weekend a crew
removed the remains of the old church while the new church
proudly stood in the background. I thought, 'This is
prophetic of the church building business.' Around the world
God is demolishing old structures while he constructs new
ones. He wants us to get into the blessing business but also go
beyond to the building business.

Getting, but Going Beyond the Blessing

Is your church a place where God's presence and power are
central – where God's River flows toward revival? This is

often intensified as thousands of churches and Christians have experienced God's blessing in renewal. We experience blessing at different levels but our hearts cry for more. Even though we get we must also go beyond 'the blessing.' We'll need a commitment **to balancing the Word and the Spirit**. Smith Wigglesworth prophesied years ago that when the Word and the Spirit came together there would be a revival world-wide such as the world has not seen up until now. Renewal of the Spirit must be grounded and governed by the Word. We can't build churches on renewal alone. We need a radical balance of both.

We should nurture our churches on the meat and potatoes of balanced church life. This will include getting soaked in Scripture, living a life of prayer, using our minds, emotions and bodies in passionate worship, getting equipped for our ministries and helping and interceding for hurting people through healing and small groups. This means that we'll do our part to train or encourage our kids and teens to be 'sold out' for Jesus. Finally, it means we'll pursue radical holiness as we give our faith away to lost people. Renewal fires will ignite life in the structures and programs of our churches. These are the makings of a revived church.

A **revived church** is a goal for renewal. To renew is 'to make new again.' It's not merely about experiencing more of the Spirit or moving in spiritual gifts (though these are included). A revived church might experience holy laughter, but it will emphasize a holy lifestyle. It might exalt the Lord with emotion and raised hands, but it will fear the Lord with devotion and raised hearts. It might have people slain in the Spirit, but it will help people become sanctified by the Spirit. A revived church will go to the wall for the Word as much as it will go to the carpet for the Spirit. It will balance exposition with experience. However, the task raises the age-old problem of wineskins.

The Problem of Wineskins

Jesus asserted that,

> '*Neither do men pour new wine into old wineskins. If they do, the skins will burst, the wine will run out and the*

wineskins will be ruined. No, they pour new wine into new wineskins, and both are preserved.' (Matthew 9:17)

As we enter the 21st century what we did in the 20th century will not necessarily work. Our old wineskins (church structures) will not contain the new wine (the Holy Spirit). Trouble happens when new wine is poured into old wineskins. The new wine is wasted. Churches must build new wineskins (containers) as they welcome new wine (*charisma*). Bottom line: in spite of fear, insecurity, and potential conflict, they must change and take risks. To reach this generation as relevant forces in the hands of God, our churches must re-tool their programs and practices whilst maintaining the message. We'll need entirely new packages, language and creativity to accomplish what King David did. After *'David had served God's purpose in his own generation, he fell asleep'* (Acts 13:36).

God does new things (cf. Isaiah 42:9; 43:19; 65:17; Ezekiel 11:19; Hebrews 10:20; Revelation 21:5). But we usually try to conserve our safe traditions rather than launch out with risky changes. Church can no longer be confined to an 11:00 am until noon service on Sundays with singing, announcements, pastoral prayer and then a sermon, followed by a Wednesday night prayer or Bible Study. These wineskins served the wine of the past. I suggest that **the problem of wineskins is more a problem of out-dated mind-sets than out-dated methods**. All revived churches and leaders – past and present – know the principle of adapting our church methods and mind-sets to reach contemporary society. John Wesley took the Gospel from inside dingy Anglican churches to the crisp outdoors to reach coal miners at 5:00 am. Martin Luther translated the Latin Bible into common German and wrote Christian lyrics set to bar-room tunes to reach his audience. William Booth set sacred words to secular songs during his Salvation Army days to reach the people of East End London. Methodist circuit riders preached from town to town on horseback and started tent-meetings (camp meetings) to reach the frontier pioneers and country folk.

I'm convinced there are no models to follow! We can't copy each other. Our stuff rarely transfers over. We can't 'franchise' our churches. We must forge into new territory as churches in our own context, in our own communities as the Spirit shows us. To survive, we must be open to creativity that will stretch us beyond our comfort zones – like our kids do with their appearance, their friends and their music. We must deal with creating stable organization with spontaneous life – fireplaces and flames.

The Fireplace and the Flame

Charles Hummel in his invigorating book, *Fire in the Fireplace*, defines a problem that plagues all churches: the relationship between organization and the life it's supposed to nurture. He writes:

> 'Throughout church history the flame in many organizational fireplaces has flickered and died. Though the fireplace was designed initially to foster a blaze, accumulations of soot eventually clogged the flue and smothered the fire.
>
> So the rekindlers of the flame are tempted – or sometimes forced – to move their fire out into the middle of the floor. At that point one of two things is likely to happen to it: either the fire rages out of control or its isolated coals die down for lack of a proper hearth. Samuel Shoemaker was right: the best place for a fire is in the fireplace, even when it calls for cleaning and remodeling.'[2]

Revived churches must be in the fireplace business. We must know how to select and build up-to-date church structures (fireplaces) that will best capture and contain the new moves of the Spirit (flames). We must see the church in charismatic not in institutional ways.

I remember sitting in Holy Trinity Brompton, an Anglican church in London that must be about 300 years old. It has big white pillars, a deep altar area, stained glass windows and a narrow sanctuary and balcony. What astounded me was how well they installed a stage and sound system, television monitors and use a full worship band all set within this archaic building. Past and present merge but they are limited by their physical structure. By the way, the Holy Spirit was there big time as the worship, preaching and prayer ministry invigorated my spirit. Perhaps they were an institutional church, but I saw little signs of it now because they understand current life in the Spirit. The new wine of renewal in the people is in contrast to the building of a past wineskin.

The New Testament Church focused on *charismata* (gifts), community, and organism. The 20th century Church tends to focus on charismatic leaders, sterile committees and rigid organization. It fixates on structure rather than Spirit. It's largely pulpit and program centered. Just look at our churches. Most of them have fixed pews and pulpits. How do we move them if new things begin to happen? Structures matter. Try changing your Sunday school or youth program. Or just try changing the format of the service. Why can't we have preaching at the beginning in preparation for a worship response at the end? We've done that at our church with great results.

Perhaps you took pride in your great Sunday school or youth ministry. You might fondly remember when people packed your evening services, or when your evangelism program brought in many converts. Or because of growth, you dedicated your new church building that now seems hopelessly old fashioned and worn out. What happened? Maybe you're still doing church the way you did it in the 70s or 80s but you now have a 90s clientele. Things change. Even successful McDonald's changed – they now serve pizza, salad, muffins, and low-fat frozen yogurt shakes. Our churches must be current in a changing culture.

The Times They Are a Changin'

Remember Bob Dylan's song of the 60s, *'The Times They Are a Changin'?'* Indeed they still are. In their book *In Search of Excellence*, Peters and Waterman studied forty-three top American companies to determine what made them successful. Two years after the book came out, fourteen of those companies faced financial trouble. Why? According to *Business Week* magazine, 'failure to react and respond to change.' In 1879 the marketing concept of the F.W. Woolworth

Company became very successful. By 1993 almost half of their 800 stores had closed. Their problem is that they could not let go of their past to serve their present customers. Likewise, the unchanging church will be unable to draw in new members and will continue to lose its youth, which feel the church has no answers. The end result is that these churches will be extinct by the time the emerging post-modern generation comes into maturity.[3] A lesson for 21st century churches is that 'yesterday's successes are no guarantee for tomorrow's survival.'[4] What changes do we face?

We don't have to look far. My wife and I recently watched the Best of the Ed Sullivan Show video series. What a hoot! In the music and entertainment industry we've come a long way baby! From the simplicity of the early Beatles and Julie Andrews to the complexity of today's Pearl Jam and Madonna. Western culture has changed drastically. We have more single-parent families, more families where both parents work, more denominations dealing with the issue of gay ordination, more retired people and those on welfare. We face more abortions, more people watching increasing hours of television each day with more stations to choose from. More teen suicide, more ethnic groups and pluralism affecting our communities and more competition for people's time than ever. In light of the present the Church faces a very interesting future. We must, as the men of Issachar, *'understand the times and know what we should do'* (1 Chronicles 12:32).[5]

21st Century Post-modern Turmoil

The Modern period of Western culture (AD 1500 to the 1960s) has been shaped largely by The Enlightenment. The Enlightenment world-view is an intellectual one that places reason and science over revelation and faith in God. It's an attempt to be free of a divinely ordered universe. Its catch phrase is 'I think, therefore I am.' But today, our culture is retreating from the intellectualism and individualism of the Modern world to the Post-modern world of relationship, community, feeling and experience. Its catch phrase might be, 'I belong, therefore I am.'[6] Enlightenment beliefs value truth and the individual while Post-modern beliefs value preference and community. To be relevant, 21st century churches must get 'back to the future.'

Casey Stengel intoned, 'The future ain't what it used to be.' Trends analyst Faith Popcorn writes, 'We have to see the future to deal with the present.' [7] Our culture is changing. Sociologists call this time a 'socioquake' because of dramatic social shake-ups. Present trends provide a social compass for the trip into the future. For example, the 21st century church faces a generational crisis with at least four distinct generations:

1. **The Builders** (1910–1946). They are stable and sacrificial. They lived though two world wars and the Great Depression. They hold traditional values.

2. **The Boomers** (1946–1964). They are the largest generation in history – 30% of the population. They are the Woodstock and Vietnam counter-culture, 'anti-establishment' materialistic, achievers.

3. **The Busters** (1965–1984). Often called 'Generation X' they are the kids of boomers and are generally pessimistic and purposeless. They come from broken homes and blended families and value relationships, media, cyberspace, immediacy and the body – how it looks and feels. They are the first truly post-modern generation.

4. **The Bridgers** (1984 onwards). This is the second largest generation living – 27% of the population. They are the 'bridge' to the 21st century and will be the dominant adult population and leaders for at least half of the next century. They are confident, optimistic, ambitious and 'religious.' Churches face enormous generational challenges for the 21st century.

Our society is in turmoil. People are losing their moral and spiritual moorings. They can't refer backward in order to extend forward. They don't have stable reference points or roots. Family, community, vocation, nationalism, religious tradition, shared values, and respect for institutions is up for grabs. This generation has no 'meta-narrative' – a life play with a central plot. All the big faiths, philosophies, ideologies, technologies and 'isms' have collapsed. There is no objective morality, no loyalty to long-standing companies, churches, or concerns, and no national dream. Personal choice empowers this generation.

Through it all, people still have 'eternity in their hearts.' In this age of mysticism, people are seeking religion and spiritual experience. They want to be spiritually 'anchored' in the past to be secure in the future. In the US, *Self* magazine conducted a study and discovered that 84% of those polled believed that a higher power listens to and answers prayer. 76% believed in miracles, 63% in life after death, 55% in ESP, 51% in Satan, 46% in 'out of body' experiences and 39% said they had 'personally experienced or witnessed a miracle.'[8] People are looking for something. They need a sturdy spiritual foundation to give meaning and order to their lives. Church attendance is soaring and more people attend church than all sporting events combined.[9] Christian influence is even getting into the business world. Laurie Beth Jones, President of an American advertizing and marketing firm wrote the best-selling book, *Jesus CEO: Using Ancient Wisdom for Visionary Leadership*.

Says Faith Popcorn,

> 'Whatever a person's specific spiritual click, one thing is evident: *we're all at the start of a great awakening, a time of spiritual and religious revival*. What's different about this awakening is that there's very little agreement on who or what God is, what constitutes worship and what this outpouring means for the future of our civilization. We're trying to put passion and meaning back into our everyday lives, to get in touch with the old values – faith, hope and charity [love].'[10]

The church has a strategic opportunity. How she responds to this spiritual foment and interest is vital to its very existence and relevance in the next millennium. For as G.K. Chesterton noted in his later life, 'Once a man stops believing in God, he does not believe in nothing – he believes in anything.'[11]

Revived Churches Will Change

Institutional Christendom is over. Apart from cultural changes, revived churches will change their own organiza-tional values and vision so they can thrive and grow with the life of Christ at the center. They won't seek to 'franchise' themselves with a uniform pattern or practice. Rather they will be portable, unpredictable, innovative and somewhat 'out of control.' They will truly exhibit 'spontaneous expansion.' They will change from running like a modern **organizational** 'reformed' church to that of a post-modern **organic** 'revived' church outlined below.

The modern organizational reformed churches of the 20th century	The post-modern organic revived churches of the 21st century
• Rigid denominational loyalty and see themselves as a church in competition with other churches in the city	• Relate to other denominations and see themselves as a church in co-operation with other churches in the city
• Largely **believe** God only **did** miracles	• Largely **behaves** as if God **does** miracles
• Institutional, audio, and spectating, with God's presence **mediated** through the clergy and liturgy	• Entrepreneurial, sensory, and participating with God's presence **immediate** through the church and the arts
• Ministry restricted to pastors and programs with a value on uniformity	• Ministry released to people and process with a value on diversity and unity
• Emphasis on individual volunteerism	• Emphasis on team ministry
• Static and maintaining as a 'bounded set' of values focused on 'chronos' time	• Spontaneous and emerging as a 'centered set' of values focused on 'kairos' time
• Values leaders in a hierarchy with titled positions and top down styles and structure	• Values leaders who model the way with integrity, synergy and Spirit

• Centralized control system which protects what God **did** in fear and closedness	• Decentralized ecosystem which processes what God is **doing** in faith and openness
• Dominated more by Greek thinking, cognitive learning and influenced by an Enlightenment worldview	• Dominated more by Hebrew thinking, relational learning and influenced by a post-modern worldview
• Emphasis on Bible knowledge, **doing**, mind and orthodoxy – 'right belief'	• Emphasis on Bible experience, **being**, heart and orthopraxy – 'right behavior'
• Emphasis on 'Teaching' and committee	• Emphasis on 'Fathering' and community
• Male dominated	• Co-partnered with women

An emerging area where revived churches of the new millennium will change is the way in which they value and bless men and women to co-partner in ministry. This is not about Christian feminism or the ordination of women. It is about men and women blessing God's original plan for mankind as He Himself blessed it. The Bible declares,

> *'God created man* [mankind] *in his own image, in the image of God he created him; male and female he created them. God blessed them and said to them, "Be fruitful and increase in number; fill the earth and subdue it." '*
>
> (Genesis 1:27–28)

Men and women are co-partners as image-bearers of God Himself and both bring essential characteristics to the human race. However, our culture and churches are largely male-dominated. But God Himself embodies male **and** female characteristics in His personality though He is neither male nor female. He is Spirit. Furthermore, not one spiritual gift in the New Testament is confined to men or women – they are available to both. Revived churches will embrace men and women functioning as the body of Christ who are being renewed in the image of God (Colossians

3:10). I'd like to say more here, but can't because of space limitations. You can read entire books on this subject.

Perhaps we need to start a 'change reaction' in our churches. Unless they change and relinquish 'control' modern institutional churches will die on the vine. Church analysts Easum and Bandy agree. In their provocative book *Growing Spiritual Redwoods*, they write,

> 'The issue of "control" dominates the agendas of the disappearing institutional churches. Church organizations are in constant anxiety about their inability to ensure responsible behavior by leaders and participants, and about their inability to match the frantic pace of cultural change. The issue of control is fueled by the desire to preserve and protect the great and glorious heritage of their institutions ... These church bureaucracies are machines with a "control center" that directs the activities of the machine.' [12]

Our churches easily fall into the pattern of doing things the way we've always done them. Like someone said, 'If you always do what you've always done, you'll always get what you've always got.' We may actually place a greater emphasis on the wineskin. For example, 'If we worship like a renewal church (of four years ago) we will be one.' Or, 'If we memorize our healing model we will experience that.' But the essence of a revived church is listening to God for **today's** agenda and listening to the culture to understand **today's** needs in light of the future. Too frequently we try to fix and manage the past instead of daring to forge and manage the future. In *Teaching Elephants to Dance*, author James A. Belasco writes about this reality concerning organizations he has consulted and managed:

> 'My experience tells me that organizations are like elephants – they both learn through conditioning. Trainers shackle young elephants with heavy chains to deeply embedded stakes. In that way the elephant learns to stay in its place. Older elephants never try to leave even though they have the strength to pull the stake and move beyond. Their conditioning limits their

movements with only a small metal bracelet around their foot – attached to nothing. Like powerful elephants, many companies are bound by earlier conditioned constraints. "We've always done it this way" is as limiting to an organization's progress as the unattached chain around the elephant's foot.' [13]

Churches must be ever living and learning, evaluating and improving. They must organize, act and evaluate. Steven Covey remarks, 'This living and learning cycle is in the spirit of *kaizen* – the Japanese word for the spirit of continuous improvement. It is in direct contrast to the Western mentality of "If it ain't broke don't fix it!"' [14] The goal of continuous church improvement is not to tear down or show disdain for denominational distinctives or time-tested values we embraced in the 20th century. For as Hummel exhorts, 'The custodians of the fireplace have the responsibility to preserve the lessons of the past – traditions of biblical principles and practices that have stood the test of time.' [15] G.K. Chesterton also stated, 'Tradition is the living faith of those now dead. Traditionalism is the dead faith of those now living.' [16]

What Are Revived Churches for the 21st Century?

According to a Gallup poll two out of three Americans believe the United States is in a serious, long-term decline, not only economically, but more importantly, morally and spiritually. Furthermore, Gallup found that one third of Americans have reported having a 'religious insight or awakening that has changed the direction of their life.' Fifty-five percent of Americans believe dealing with the transcendent will play a much greater role in their lives as they enter the new millennium. [17]

People long for deep spiritual experience. They want hair-raising experiences. Don't you? We gotta get past dead orthodoxy, bland mediocrity, and cultural irrelevance if we hope to satisfy people's spiritual needs. Sometimes stodgy Christians can be like the guy who asked his friend the question 'What's worse, ignorance or apathy?' His friend's reply: 'I don't know and I don't care.' Perhaps a prophetic statement was made to the Church when the hippie wrote on a poster back in the 60s 'Jesus is the Answer, but What's the Question?'

While the majority of Canadians, Americans and the British say they believe in God, most want nothing to do with the Church or organized religion. Most denominations have plateaued or are losing people and almost all the mainline churches are dying. People want God but don't want church. The Church (especially in the Western world) is largely powerless. Bill Bright declares that 'having fallen into the cult of the comfortable, the Church, for the most part, is no longer a power to be reckoned with.'[18] He goes on to say that,

> 'According to numerous surveys, fifty percent of the hundred million who attend church each Sunday have no assurance of their salvation and ninety-five percent are not familiar with the Person and ministry of the Holy Spirit. Only two percent of believers in America regularly share their faith with others. The reality of God seems far removed from everyday life ... For a great many Christians, God is a mental concept to consider on Sunday morning. Indeed, the chief sin in the Church today is unbelief. It is impossible to be "on fire" for God when He is not real to you.'[19]

As David Bryant asks, 'How do we prepare for AD 2000 and beyond?' Below is his reply:

> 'Among the many options presented, none are being stressed more strongly at the moment than what futurologists say is the single greatest hope for human survival: what happens to the human spirit. Increasingly, hope for the human race is ultimately pinned on a spiritual and moral renaissance more than anything else.'[20]

What do I mean by a revived church? *Webster's Dictionary* defines the word 'revive' as, 'to return to consciousness, or life; to recover life, vigor, or strength; to become reanimated or reinvigorated, to become active, operative, valid, or flourishing again.' A revived church is one that is conscious, lively, invigorating, active, operative, valid, restored and flourishing. It's a church where the *dunamis* (power) of the Holy Spirit is released (see Luke 4:14; 5:17; Acts 1:8; 6:8; 10:38; Romans 15:19; 1 Corinthians 2:4; Ephesians 3:16). This word *dunamis* is where we get the words 'dynamite' and 'dynamic' from. Where the Holy Spirit lives you will find lively, dynamic, and powerful results. It's where people will say, 'Man, I can't wait to get to church. I love it. God is there. I don't know what's going to happen next. I'm blown away!' This is an **empowered church**. It embraces 'the seasons of revival' and experiences God's empowering presence as it creatively balances Word and Spirit, structure and spontaneity.

A revived church is *'being built together to become a dwelling in which God lives by his Spirit'* (Ephesians 2:22). It's 'saturated with God.' God can revive dusty Anglican, Baptist, Mennonite, Catholic, Presbyterian, Methodist, Vineyard, or Pentecostal churches. I don't want to feel like a corpse in church? Do you? Well, let's echo the following passages for our churches as we seek to deliver what's listed in our bulletins.

> *'Then we will not turn away from you; revive us, and we will call on your name. Restore us, O Lord God Almighty; make your face shine upon us, that we may be saved.'*
> (Psalm 80:18–19)

> *'Will you not revive us again, that your people may rejoice in you?'* (Psalm 85:6)

> *'Come, let us return to the Lord. He has torn us to pieces but he will heal us; he has injured us but he will bind up our wounds. After two days he will revive us; on the third day he will restore us, that we may live in his presence. Let us acknowledge the Lord; let us press on to acknowledge him. As surely as the sun rises, he will appear; he will come to us like the winter rains, like the spring rains that water the earth.'* (Hosea 6:1–3)

Chapter 2

The Art of Leadership and Renewal

*'A leader is one who knows the way, goes the way,
and shows the way.'*
(John Maxwell)

For the past ten years or so, I've been consumed with the topic of leadership. Before then I gave it little thought. I thought about teaching, preaching, pastoring, and administrating. By 1983, I had logged four strenuous years at Dallas Theological Seminary training to become a church leader for full-time ministry. The mission of the seminary is 'to prepare men and women for ministry as godly servant-leaders in the body of Christ world-wide.' But at seminary I never took one course nor read one book on leadership. Yet in ministry, I enter situations where Greek and Hebrew, expository preaching, theology and church history do not necessarily help me lead people. I have seen that leaders spend most of their time dealing with seven major 'P's': People, Problems, Putting out fires, Pain in people's lives, Planning, Paperwork and the need for Perseverance. They also log much time in meetings to deal with the 'big seven.' I've concluded that 'leadership is tough and then you die!'

The Art of Leadership

I believe that **pastoring** a church and **leading** a church are very different assignments. I now want to become a more effective leader as well as pastor. Through mistakes and musings I have become aware of the screaming need for another 'P': Principle-centered leadership – where godly principles coupled with goodly practices pave the way for fruitful influence. Read this simple yet profound principle in Judges 5:2,

> 'When the princes in Israel take the lead, when the people willingly offer themselves – praise the LORD!'

When the leaders lead, the followers willingly follow and the result is 'Praise the Lord!' Now that's artful leadership!

Renewal and Revival

For the past ten years or so, I have also been consumed with the topic of renewal and of late, revival. For a decade, I've been a member of the pastoral leadership team here at New Life, first as an elder, then as Associate Senior Pastor and now as Senior Pastor. In 1986 I joined this conservative evangelical church plant as a founding member with Wesley Campbell, David Ruis and others. We all had a heart for church renewal. I had developed a seminar on principles of church renewal that helped forge our philosophy of ministry. Dr Gene Getz and Frank Tillapaugh were writers who shaped our thinking.[21] Our new church was vibrant and open to the Holy Spirit, but for us Baptists and Brethren, church renewal was mainly being 'contemporary' and flex-ible in our forms, governed by the four vital functions of worship, nurture, community and mission. That set the tone for Holy Spirit renewal to come.

We had also shed our anti-supernatural backgrounds, as we believed that all the gifts of the Spirit were for today. When we experienced our first visitation of God in 1987–1988, we knew little about renewal through the manifest presence of the Spirit in supernatural gifts and manifesta-tions of His presence. We were also novices in how to intelligently lead people in and through renewal.[22] God 're-arranged our domes' and changed our theologies. Because we had to lead people in renewal and beyond, it forced us to deal with the subject of leadership.

In the last couple of years this 'season of revival' has gripped our hearts. One day our pastoral team was having an all-day planning meeting and we gathered at a restaurant for lunch to discuss our vision. I looked at Wesley Campbell and the others and asked, 'Hey guys, what's our vision, where are we going?' It was clear that we did not know. Leaders without a vision wander and the people wonder. As we talked I think I had what some might call a 'word of wisdom.' I retorted, 'I know what our ultimate vision is, it's revival.' A small seed was sown. But revival requires leaders and people that will balance Spirit and structure, charisma and container.

Balancing Charisma and Container

There are many books and seminars on how to manage and grow a church. Many of these have to do with administration, not leadership. I know it's difficult to integrate a move of the Holy Spirit with a program, plan, or structure unless He is part of them. Revived churches will balance Spirit and structure, pioneering and homesteading, charisma and container. The following chart illustrates what I mean:

Spirit	Structure
Let the River Flow	Keep the Banks of the River
Organism (Life)	Organization (Structure)
Function	Form
Letting it Fly Freely	Flying it with Freedom
Electricity	Wires
Pioneering	Homesteading [23]
Freedom	Limits
Prophecy and Revelation	Interpretation and Application
Body Life	Body Parts
Charisma (Content)	Container (Cup)

Dr Margaret Poloma, in a groundbreaking study, shows how the Assemblies of God have endangered their ability to carry on their beginnings in *charisma* (Spirit, experience, miraculous) with present institutionalism (structure, organization, bureaucracy). She states, 'Although religion in its best form requires both organization and personal experience, Maslow contended that much institutionalized religion quickly loses sight of the religious experience that generated it.'[24] In other words, people can have a religious experience which over time can settle into habits, rituals, and legalism. The founders who began with the Spirit are forgotten by the followers who transform the movement into an institution. Ever seen that? I have.

Consider the present state of only a few denominations such as the Quakers, Methodists and Christian and Missionary Alliance. They all began with charisma, the supernatural, and a charismatic leader. Generally, however, their charismatic roots and experiences today lie dormant in history books. This also happened to the early church. What began with charisma in the Book of Acts grew into institutionalism with Catholicism by the middle of the fourth century AD. This also tends to happen to individual churches. They begin in the Spirit but end in institutionalism. We must cultivate Spirit and structure, function and form.

What someone values in the name of 'Spirit' is *sometimes* a projection of their right-brained personality-type. Some of these people are more intuitive, spontaneous, and can be resistant to 'structure,' boundaries, or being accountable. I've seen people resist and resent 'structure' in their sometimes misguided (and even rebellious) attempts to let the Holy Spirit have his way and not quench that 'freedom.' Some of these people have unhealthy problems with leaders and authority. Some are fear-based and controlling. Remember, **leadership and administration are also spiritual gifts of the Holy Spirit** (cf. Romans 12:8; 1 Corinthians 12:28).

Spirit with little structure ultimately causes confusion and consternation in people. You cannot release a torrent of prophecy, words of knowledge, unhindered worship and unmonitored preaching or praying to freely take their own course. Freedom needs 'order.' Dr Clark Pinnock remarks that, 'Freedom needs order and order needs freedom in the church. We need neither a supercharged church without discipline nor a lifeless church without Spirit. Renewal needs wise oversight to protect it from abuse. It needs leaders who encourage and supervise the ministries of the laity. Such leaders benefit the body when they are visionary and create room for the Spirit.' [25]

We need Spirit structure and administration. Pioneers must eventually homestead and we must organize experiential chaos. Read what Rick Warren says about this as he compares two revivalists of the 18th century – George Whitefield and John Wesley:

> 'Whitefield was best known for his preaching. In his lifetime, he preached over 18,000 sermons, averaging ten a week! ... However, biographers have pointed out that Whitefield's work often left his converts without any organization so the results of his work were of short duration. Today, very few Christians would recognize George Whitefield's name. In contrast, John Wesley's name is still recognized by millions of Christians. Why is this? Wesley was an itinerant preacher just like Whitefield, ... But Wesley was also an organizer. He created an organizational structure to fulfill his purpose that far outlasted his lifetime. That organization is called the Methodist Church! For any renewal to last in a church, there must be a structure to nurture and support it.' [26]

A challenge for tomorrow's church today is to both construct fireplaces (structure, organization) and stoke the flames (Spirit, organism). How do you know when you have achieved the balance? When the **Word is emphasized and the fruit of the Spirit is evident** through **servanthood**, governed by **faith**, **hope**, **love** and **walking** and being **led** by the Spirit with an openness that leads to freedom.

> *'Where the Spirit of the Lord is, there is freedom.'*
> (2 Corinthians 3:17)

(See also fuller treatments in Romans and Galatians 5.)

How do we do this? For starters by valuing spontaneity – hey it's OK if some things happen which make us feel uncomfortable. Later in Chapter 11 I'll talk about 'open church.' Develop listening prayer and waiting, intuition and discernment – yeah, you can trust your 'hunches,' feelings and 'checks.' Allow prophecy – yes, God does speak through people not just through the Bible and circumstances. Take faith risks – when God tells you to jump off the diving board into an empty swimming pool and promises to fill it up on your way down! Get creative – let your imagination run rampant as it pushes the boundaries of rigid thinking. Then 'let go and let God.' God seems to work as much in the subjective as in the objective. However, most Western Christians aren't taught to value or trust the subjective. It's possible, but there will be agony and ecstasy.

The Agony and the Ecstasy

Watching the Olympics we've all seen the agony of defeat and the ecstasy of victory. Renewal is an adventure of agony and ecstasy, of losing and winning, of conflict and change requiring steady character. Three challenges face revived churches: **managing conflict**, **motivating change**, and **modeling character**. The Holy Spirit causes change while tensions mount. The initial effect is often conflict and sometimes division. More battles are fought over change than theology. Most of us don't like change. We like a safe environment. Why do tongues, holy laughter, people shaking, prophecy, and words of knowledge cause so much trouble? Because they jar people's emotions and theologies. We need godly character and faith to see us through.

Most of us fall into one of four tendencies in our personality types. As we understand how we are made and see how others are made, we can become more effective in

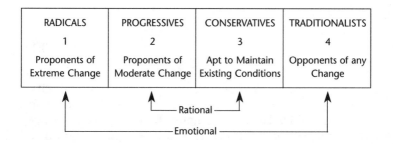

RADICALS	PROGRESSIVES	CONSERVATIVES	TRADITIONALISTS
1	2	3	4
Proponents of Extreme Change	Proponents of Moderate Change	Apt to Maintain Existing Conditions	Opponents of any Change

Rational

Emotional

dealing with our conflicts as we work together to become revived churches.[27]

1. **Radicals** are the sources of many good ideas and provide 'leavening' in the dough mix. They tend to be impulsive and at times unwise. They operate in an emotional climate. They are early starters with quick burnout who help get the rocket off the ground like a booster. They will help motivate and empower change. Radicals push the envelope and look like 'rebels.' They can threaten conservatives and traditionalists. They say, 'Let's go for it.'

2. **Progressives** are tuned into and anticipate the need for change. They are risk-takers who live on the edge but are not hasty. They operate in a rational climate. They quickly perceive the benefits in good planning and will spearhead new directions. Old programs do not interest them and they are the best communicators to the conservatives. They will provide spirit and stability in change. They say, 'Let's go for it, but let's slow down.'

3. **Conservatives** see the value of the status quo and do not have a felt-need for change. Many of them join a church because it satisfies their needs. They will anger the progressives and radicals because they ask the strategic questions that those groups did not think to ask. They will be a ballast for a 'ship of fools' to keep them honest and balanced. They operate in a rational climate and are not hasty. Financially, they give the most. Radicals don't have it and progressives don't keep it. They say, 'Well maybe let's go, but why do we have to?'

4. **Traditionalists** are extremely resistant to change and have a tendency to be hostile, angry and vocal about change. They will complain and argue. Although they sound rational, they operate in an emotional climate. Progressives perceive them as enemies or obstacles. They do not support change and in the rare case where they do, they will not want the change changed. They say, 'I don't want to go.'

Can you see yourself generally in one of the above categories? Do you see how you can be a help or a hindrance to God-inspired change which causes conflict as you work with the other types? Churches predominantly fall into one of these four categories as well. Remember, 'we never did it way that before' **cannot** be our motto. Radicals and progressives might lead revived churches but they need conservatives and traditionalists to support them – that's where most people are at. Because fear and comfort form the root of resistance to change, we must:

1. Define the vision.
2. Sell the problems.
3. Go slowly when moving fast. Someone said, 'Go slow. Churches are a lot like horses. They don't like to be startled or surprised. It causes deviant behavior.'
4. Be person-centered rather than program-centered.
5. Provide many opportunities for dialogue, communication, and teaching.
6. Garner ownership from the core leaders and opinion-maker's first.
7. Manage transitions, as we help people let go of what was as they struggle in the neutral zone of what will be.[28] French novelist André Gide declared, 'One doesn't discover new lands without consenting to lose sight of the shore for a very long time.'

Welcoming Renewal into Your Church

If we can help each other gain a biblical and practical framework, we will more easily align our beliefs with our experience and will change. I wrote *Let the River Flow: Welcoming Renewal Into Your Church* to help people deal with the issues of conflict and change in the current renewal. In our churches we can make the mistake of sometimes focusing too much on manifestations, prophecy, renewal and revival. We gotta be real not just religious. We still have to go to work, parent our children and deal with our frustrations and pain. We are still called to be 'saints of the daily grind.'

Just this afternoon I received a call from a woman. She was staying at a motel with her daughter – teary, desperate and crying for help. She felt 'led' to call me for prayer and counsel. Her 31st anniversary was two days away, but she had lost any feelings for her husband and for the Lord. She had not been to church in a year but had been to several renewal conferences to 'catch the fire.' She said that she couldn't find a renewal church where she lives. Maybe she caught the fire but what good is that if she lost the flame of love for her husband and her Lord? She then appeared on her anniversary with her husband and daughter at one of our renewal meetings. During the ministry time I saw her shake under the power of the Spirit. But I wonder: after she goes back home and the shaking stops will she be any different?

What is Leadership?

I define leadership with one word, **influence**. Leadership is about influencing people. We are all leaders to a certain degree. You lead other people as you influence them. Someone estimated that an ordinary person influences 10,000 people in a lifetime. Leadership is not about administration or management. It's not about position, title or authority. It's about contagious vision, character, and example. Jim Wallis of the Sojourners community once wrote: 'The only way to propagate a message is to live it.'

Once I was talking with Colorado pastor James Ryle. As we talked, he shared some principles about leadership. He said, 'Leadership is action.' Leaders will act when they have a target or a destination. They thrive on vision and values. Vision is where they are going and values are why they are going there. But the basic question is – is their target or vision the right one? Leaders must answer the following five core questions:
1.   Where am I going?
2.   Why am I going there?
3.   Who told me to do it?
4.   What has God called me to do?
5.   How am I to do it?

Has God called you? Without answers to these questions, confusion and ineffectiveness result. This is true in too many churches. Let's become 'people of action.'

We need to learn the art of following and serving if we

expect the river to flow through our influence. Tiorio wrote, 'You will never be a leader unless you first learn to follow and be led.' Robert Greenleaf declared, 'Good leaders must first become good servants.' James Ryle's son, David, said a very insightful thing, 'Everyone likes to talk about being a servant until they are treated like one.' Someone said, 'If you pray – "Lord use me" – you can't then later say, "I feel used."' Promotion comes from the Lord (Psalm 75:7). 'Leadership,' exhorts Max Depree, 'is much more an art, a belief, a condition of the heart, than a set of things to do.'

The Qualifications of Leaders for the 21st Century

The changes in culture and church in the 21st century will require changes for leaders and people. Leith Anderson remarks, 'The twenty-first century will require some new types of leaders. Peter Drucker says every time an organization doubles in size, half of the leadership becomes obsolete. I am a leader and I fear obsolescence.'[29] Leith goes on to list what he believes are the qualifications of leaders for the 21st century church:[30]

– **Attuned to their culture**. It is not enough to know our Bible. We must know our culture and our people.
– **Flexible**. Rigid people with inflexible methods are going to bend and break in the years ahead.
– **Relational**. Churches want leaders who are real and approachable.
– **Good communicators**. We need people like Abraham Lincoln and Winston Churchill who can communicate the vision and move people.
– **Entrepreneurs**. The ability to make something succeed. To see opportunities in the changes and strategize to turn these into good for God's kingdom.
– **Risk takers**. Willing to fail in order to succeed.
– **Godly**. Those who have Christian integrity, who have suffered enough to be tested and proven. Those who have their prayers answered. Remember, 'what you can build with your gifting you can destroy with your character.'

Character is forged more than given. Get used to the heat, the hammer, and the anvil. Choose godly character before good gifting.

What Are Renewal and Revival?

As I write about leadership in 'renewal' and 'revival,' I know people define these terms differently. There is structural and spiritual renewal. Structural renewal might involve using new songs, re-arranging the seating in the sanctuary, having small groups, developing a less liturgical service, practicing 'body life,' or lay-leaders doing more of the ministry, and so on.

However, I'm talking about spiritual renewal – where we welcome the Holy Spirit and where we grant Him freedom to run our churches, programs, services and lives. I do not equate renewal with manifestations and phenomena. To renew means 'to make new again, to replenish, to revive.' Biblical renewal is God's presence and power through His Word and His Spirit, imparting new life and spiritual fruit in His people. It's a greater openness to the Spirit. Dr Clark Pinnock describes renewal this way,

> 'The Spirit, who is already present in the believer, becomes present in a new way. God becomes more real: there is a greater sense of His presence, an increase in power to bear witness, a greater openness to and manifestation of gifts. What was previously intellectual becomes experiential. The indwelling of the Spirit is experienced in a conscious way (Galatians 5:25; Ephesians 3:16–17). We experience enlightenment, taste the heavenly gift and the goodness of the word of God, and discover powers of the age to come (Hebrews 6:4–5).' [31]

What is revival? There are many definitions. Basically it's the revitalizing of saints in the church together with the awakening of sinners outside the church resulting in social impact and the advance of God's kingdom in communities and countries. Revival brings back to life that which is dead.

Summary

We can become revived churches in renewal but must go beyond to revival. Let's seek to be empowered evangelicals who endeavor to balance content (the Word and programs) with charisma (the Spirit and process). We will build fireplaces while fanning the flames.

Chapter Three

Ministry by the Spirit

'Send the Spirit now, for Jesus Christ's sake.
Send the Spirit powerfully now, for Jesus Christ's sake.
Send the Spirit more powerfully now, for Jesus Christ's sake.
Send the Spirit still more powerfully now, for Jesus Christ's sake.'
(Evan Roberts, Welsh Revivalist)

John the Baptist said to the crowds,

> *'I baptize you with water. But one more powerful than I will come... He will baptize you with the Holy Spirit and with fire.'*　　　　　　　　　　　　　　　　　　(Luke 3:16)

John Arnott, Senior Pastor of the Toronto Airport Christian Fellowship, hosts numerous 'Catch the Fire' and other conferences. He wants to impart the 'Father's Blessing' so people will 'walk in God's love and then give it away' to others. People are ignited at renewal conferences in Toronto and elsewhere around the world and then return to their locations to spread it. Then they go on crusades to share it with others – sometimes with blazing zeal without tactical knowledge. After renewal, then what? And **how**? I suggest we must first know something about fire and the Spirit.

Ministry on the Fireline

On cold winter nights, our family will sit around the fire-place, play games, have hot chocolate, talk, and stare at the fire. Strange isn't it? There's a mystique about fire. As we watch it dance and hear it hiss and pop as it radiates heat and light, fire captivates us. I've asked our children what they see. They see various colors: red, green, purple, blue and yellow. Of course, the kids aren't content to stare at it, they also want to poke at the logs. They also want to help light it, throw logs on it and then eventually play with it. Parents get nervous when their kids play with fire. Until they have enough experience with it, they can burn themselves or start something they can't control.

If we are to build fireplaces, we should have first-hand experiences with the fire of the Holy Spirit. Pentecostals and Charismatics might say, 'Brother Roger, that's nothing new. We've been saying this for years. You gotta get the baptism of the Holy Spirit and speak in tongues. Read the red and pray for the power!' But I'm not talking about a Pentecostal or Charismatic experience with a formula. I'm talking about pastors and people who regularly experience God's presence, who've tasted the powers of the coming age (Hebrews 6:5), who've felt the flames and inhaled the smoke, and who'll commit themselves to first-hand ministry on the fireline.

Dr Ray Anderson in his book *Ministry on the Fireline* discusses basic principles of fire fighting. Those in the command post deploy and give orders to those on the fireline. Firefighters must go where they are deployed not where they see flames. Firefighters trust the judgment of those at the command post as long as they themselves have felt the flames and inhaled the smoke. As one firefighter said, 'If they are only theorists and not firefighters, I have little confidence in their strategy.' After firefighters experience fires first-hand only then can they direct others in how to fight them.[32]

The Feast of Fire

We should not want the fire of the Holy Spirit if it's only the newest item on the church growth menu. I'm talking about building churches by the Spirit not a method for church growth. We can build gorgeous church buildings, have lots of parking, be seeker sensitive and run great programs, but without the Spirit we will have a nice white shell with no egg inside. For,

> *'Unless the* LORD *builds the house, its builders labor in vain.'*
> (Psalm 127:1)

God builds with sacred fire.

It's easy to become an armchair advocate of renewal by attending conferences, reading books, listening to tapes and watching from the sidelines without getting near the flames. As Anderson says, 'Fire-fighting science, I am told, is most effective when done by those whose teacher is the fire.'[33]

To minister by the Spirit we must live by the Spirit.

Living By the Spirit

Paul encouraged that,

> *'Since we live by the Spirit, let us keep in step with the Spirit.'*
> (Galatians 5:25)

The Revised English Bible translates is this way, *'If the Spirit is the source of our life, let the Spirit also direct its course.'* We cannot keep in step if we don't live by the Spirit. 'Living by the Spirit is the root; walking by the Spirit is the fruit.'[34]

How do we live by the Spirit?

To live by the Spirit is unnerving yet exciting, full of tension yet peace, with strange yet wonderful outcomes. We are open with unbridled expectation for Him to move, urge and guide, by obedient and risky faith fastened to the Father's agenda. Clark Pinnock draws the example from Jesus, 'The world did not set the agenda for Jesus. People could not predict what he would do next, because he had no plan but sought what the Father wanted. He did not operate from a program. Need alone did not constitute the divine call. He waited for God's urging and the Spirit's guiding.'[35]

I've had my paradigm challenged and my heart tenderized by God's Spirit. I've had to humble myself with tears in private and in public to lay down my crowns of competition, drive, control and insensitivity. Sometimes it was a prophetic word that brought conviction, at other times it was the Bible, a good book, correction from someone, or God's nudge in my conscience. I've come to the place where my position, my viewpoint, or whether I will preach or be a catalyst for revival is not important to me. At times I have quenched God's Spirit, causing His presence to withdraw. I have heard prophetic words that uncovered my secret thoughts. I've had some awful experiences where we went through the motions on Sunday mornings, with good content, but with no Spirit – where it felt like *Ichabod* (Hebrew for 'no glory'). The fear of God has gripped my heart. I want to choose the path of humility and brokenness. I believe this is the way of the Spirit for God's empowering presence.

As a church, lots we've done has worked. We planned great services, sponsored exciting conferences, and rallied the people to noble causes – often without much prayer or inquiring of the Lord. Until 1997, when God didn't bless as freely as He used to. What we used to do started to not work anymore. We took too much for granted. When we didn't get the same results and began to feel God's presence withdraw, you can bet our anxiety levels increased! Especially when He prophetically indicated that we were 'utilitarians.' I came to a place where I laid everything down at the altar of sacrifice, through repentance and reflection. I began to ask, 'Where is the Spirit moving, initiating, or directing? On whom is the Spirit abiding or anointing?' I had to decrease and defer, even as a senior pastor. I came to a broken place where I did not matter nearly as much. What were God's plans, who did He want to preach or lead worship on Sundays, on whom did He place His anointing to accomplish certain tasks? I felt 'demoted' to **Junior Pastor**, right where God wanted me – the low road of brokenness, submission, and servanthood. We live by the Spirit as we yield to Him, as we submit our plans, our programs, and our personal lives to the Spirit – in advance.

To live by the Spirit also means, like Jehoshaphat, that we **inquire** of the Lord,

> *'Alarmed, Jehoshaphat resolved to inquire of the* LORD, *and he proclaimed a fast for all Judah.'*   (2 Chronicles 20:3)

If you want a fertile Bible study, do a concordance search on the word 'inquire.' Note the positive and negative aspects of those that did and did not inquire of the Lord. Those who live by the Spirit inquire of the Lord. They search out the prophetic while they strategize the pastoral.

The Prophetic and the Pastoral

We've had a tough road with the prophetic – some of it personal issues between prophets and some of it philosophical and practical issues between prophets and pastors. I don't think there are trouble-free churches where the gift of prophecy flows. But it's a **significant means by which God communicates with His people**. The New Testament is clear, *'Do not despise prophecies'* (1 Thesselonians 5:20 NKJV), and *'Follow the way of love and eagerly desire spiritual gifts, especially the gift of prophecy'* (1 Corinthians 14:1). A goal of the prophetic is to communicate God's **heart**.

The prophetic works best in community and in conjunction with governmental gifts and offices as the Spirit leads into mission and ministry. The following illustrates the point,

> *'In the church at Antioch there were prophets and teachers: Barnabas, Simeon called Niger, Lucius of Cyrene, Manaen (who had been brought up with Herod the tetrarch) and Saul. While they were worshiping the Lord and fasting, the Holy Spirit said, "Set apart for me Barnabas and Saul for the work to which I have called them." So after they had fasted and prayed, they placed their hands on them and sent them off. The two of them, sent on their way by the Holy Spirit.'*
> (Acts 13:1–4)

Our pastoral team meets at least twice per month on Tuesday afternoons with several of our prophetic and intercessory leaders to submit, discuss, and pray over revelation from the Lord. This revelation can come as Scriptures, dreams, visions, verbal words, pictures, feelings, or through a variety of other revelatory means. At these meetings, we also submit strategic matters and imminent decisions to pray about and inquire of the Lord's heart and will. Perhaps you receive revelation through dreams, impressions, pictures, feelings, or words in your spirit. Work with the leaders to submit your prophetic for interpretation and application.

The prophetic role is to hear God's instruction.[36] The pastoral (governmental) role is to be accountable for God's instruction and to implement it. Prophetic people should not try to 'enforce' their revelation or control pastors with it. That's not their responsibility. Below are some key contrasts and complements between prophetic and governmental roles:

Prophetic	Governmental
1. Subjective	1. Objective
2. Volatile	2. Structural
3. Itinerant	3. Permanent
4. Functional	4. Relational
5. Intuitive	5. Logical
6. Idealistic	6. Practical
7. Spontaneous	7. Premeditative
8. Personal	8. Corporate
9. Inspirational	9. Informative
10. Creative	10. Managerial

At times, God will give revelation to the governmental first and at other times to the prophetic first. Co-operation and unity are essential. A balance of planning and spontaneity is also essential. Communication between the prophetic and the pastoral is also essential for the proper building of the church. This is a mark of a revived church – balance and harmony between the prophetic and pastoral (governmental). I've come to intercessory meetings not knowing exactly what I would preach on the next Sunday. Through prayer the Lord has given specific guidance on what was on His heart. Once, the theme of intercession centered on humility. One Sunday I spoke on 'Descending into Greatness' from Philippians 2:1–11. It had a major impact on the church. God led it, I only aligned myself under it.

More Lord?

It's easy to say, 'More Lord' but when He does will you be prepared? He might bring things that we can't handle. You might be **ready**, but are you **prepared**? – big difference. A couple of years ago a seasoned pastor visited our church with his fellow staff and elders for a weekend. He had seen renewal during his ministry but more from the charismatic renewal of the 1970s. We prayed for and prophesied over them. They were hungry for renewal in their church but weren't sure how to incorporate it. They tried praying for people, tried to release prophecy, tried contemporary worship, believed in the gifts of the Spirit, and cast vision for 'renewal.' But they couldn't get the Lord 'to show up.' The pastor saw a contrast in our church and wanted to know what our 'key' was.

I felt prompted to say to him, (we'll call him John), 'John, it's time to put all your eggs in one basket and go for it.' I sensed this pastor relished the past and had lost touch with the present. He was pastoring an older conservative though somewhat open Baptist church. He declared 'I'm open and have faith for the Spirit,' yet he acted with gentlemanly control for fear of things getting out of hand. He eventually settled back into a respectable but stymied church. Building by the Spirit is not easy. It can rattle you. Do we really want more, Lord? If so, we must go for it!

Go For It!

We've decided by faith and passion to put all our eggs into one basket, to go for it, to welcome the Spirit's leading, on His terms, in His way. It's kind of like Abraham to whom God said *'Leave your country, your people and your father's household and go to the land I will show you'* (Genesis 12:1). The Bible says that without faith it is impossible to please God (Hebrews 11:6) and difficult to release the miraculous

(Matthew 13:58). God 'shows up' more often when the door of faith and expectancy is open than He does when we use the 'right methods' or techniques.

Several years ago Gord Whyte, our Pastor of Counseling and Prayer, motivated me by his example to go for it, even at the prospect of losing face or failing. He had consistently cried out to God to release the miraculous when he prayed for people. Over time his faith grew as he successfully took risks to give people prophecies or words of knowledge and pray for healing. He would come back repeatedly and tell us at staff meetings how God used him. God would give Gord the names of people he had not met and would give him insights into people's lives that blew them away when he prophesied over them. Then Gord resolved that he would really take a risk and publicly pray for people's legs and arms to lengthen and backs to straighten. It happened. He showed me how. This began to inspire my faith to go for it.

The goal wasn't to dazzle people, it was to minister to people, to increase their faith levels and to inject the miraculous into everyday ministry. Gradually I mustered enough courage to give words of knowledge (which at first seemed like they were simply my own thoughts), deliver prophetic words (which is always difficult because you are never sure in advance if what you will say will hit the bullseye), and to pray for legs, arms, and backs. Guess what? It happened and it still happens!

I'll give you another example. Nathan, our youth pastor, invited me to speak to our Junior Youth at a weekend retreat. I asked him to give me a list of the names of all who signed up – about thirty. While praying at home, I felt a nudge to pray through the list of names one by one (most of the kids I didn't know). I also felt a nudge to **expect** God to give me a prophetic encouragement for each one. This was a stretch for me but I decided to go for it. I wrote down two or three characteristics about each person that I felt the Lord wanted to affirm. I received something for everyone except for three boys at the end of the list. I felt the Lord say that I was to pray for them on the spot at the retreat and 'get something' there. Yikes!

Well, after I spoke for about thirty minutes to the kids, I
then presented each one with what I'd received for them. As
it turned out, 99% of it was on the mark and confirmed by
others. In addition to this, the three boys were leaders and
close friends that had come for the retreat at the last minute.
The day before, our youth pastor had even grouped them
together to pray for one another. As I called for them to
come and sit in the middle of the floor, they were even
sitting together on a couch. That evening, I felt that the
youth themselves were supposed to pray for them and wait
on God for revelation. Sure enough, the Lord gave words
through many of the youth for each boy. We also prayed
similarly for a few others who were not on the list and then
for the youth leaders. We did an old fashioned 'clinic,' but it
all started with my preparation at home praying over each
youth by name and writing down the things that came to
mind. What's the key? Well, simply stated, Nike says 'Just do
it!' But do it with both the filling and the fullness of the
Spirit.

Live By the Filling and the Fullness of the Spirit

In their book *Receiving the Power*, Brad Long and Doug
McMurry point out the crucial difference between the **filling**
and **fullness** of the Spirit. They write:

> 'When the New Testament speaks of people being
> "filled with" or "full of" the Holy Spirit, the Greek
> word reveals one of two concepts ... One Greek term,
> *pleitho*, is used consistently for the outer work of the
> Holy Spirit and usually refers to a brief temporary filling.
> Another Greek word, *pleiroo* (or its cognate *pleires*), is
> used consistently for the inner work of the Holy Spirit
> and usually refers to something that gets fuller and
> fuller until it is saturated. This refers to a state of
> being.' [37]

With *pleitho* the Spirit temporarily 'comes upon' someone
to meet an immediate need resulting in an action. This

happens repeatedly. With *pleiroo*, the Spirit works 'within' someone as a state of being. This happens as an ongoing and progressive experience usually without an action, though perhaps with an attending circumstance. The difference between these words (English translations can't reflect the difference) is illustrated below:[38]

Examples of *Pleitho* not used for the Holy Spirit

*'Immediately one of them ran and got a sponge. He **filled** it with wine vinegar, put it on a stick, and offered it to Jesus to drink.'* (Matthew 27:48)

*'So they signaled their partners in the other boat to come and help them, and they came and **filled** both boats so full that they began to sink.'* (Luke 5:7)

Examples of *Pleitho* used for the Holy Spirit

*'When Elizabeth heard Mary's greeting, the baby leaped in her womb, and Elizabeth was **filled** with the Holy Spirit. In a loud voice she exclaimed.'* (Luke 1:41–42)

*'All of them were **filled** with the Holy Spirit and began to speak in other tongues as the Spirit enabled them.'* (Acts 2:4)

*'After they prayed, the place where they were meeting was shaken. And they were all **filled** with the Holy Spirit and spoke the word of God boldly.'* (Acts 4:31)

*'Then Saul, who was also called Paul, **filled** with the Holy Spirit, looked straight at Elymas.'* (Acts 13:9–10)

Examples of *Pleiroo* and *Pleires* not used for the Holy Spirit

*'And the child grew and became strong; he was **filled** with wisdom, and the grace of God was upon him.'* (Luke 2:40)

*'Then Mary took about a pint of pure nard, an expensive perfume; she poured it on Jesus' feet and wiped his feet with her hair. And the house was **filled** with the fragrance of the perfume.'* (John 12:3)

Examples of *Pleiroo* and *Pleires* used for the Holy Spirit

> *'Jesus, **full** of the Holy Spirit, returned from the Jordan and was led by the Spirit in the desert, where for forty days he was tempted by the devil.'* (Luke 4:1–2)

> *'Brothers, choose seven men from among you who are known to be **full** of the Spirit and wisdom.'* (Acts 6:3)

> *'He [Barnabas] was a good man, **full** of the Holy Spirit and faith, and a great number of people were brought to the Lord.'* (Acts 11:24)

> *'Do not get drunk on wine, which leads to debauchery. Instead, be **filled** with the Spirit. Speak to one another with psalms, hymns and spiritual songs. Sing and make music in your heart to the Lord.'* (Ephesians 5:18–19)

When the Spirit temporarily fills you (*pleitho*), you experience His outward **power** for situations of **conduct**. Have you ever surprised yourself when you prayed for someone, or led worship, or taught a Bible study and things just flowed out of you like a river? You felt boldness and power? Did you think, 'Wow, was that really me. I can't believe what I did.' Hey, that's the filling of the Spirit.

When the Spirit cultivates ongoing fullness (*pleiroo* and *pleires*), you experience His inward **presence** for situations of **character**. Filling is about gifting. Fullness is about holiness. Why was Jesus so effective? James Dunn explains, 'His awareness of being uniquely possessed and used by divine Spirit was the mainspring of his mission and the key to its effectiveness.'[39] Jesus was a charismatic person. In what sense? Again Dunn concludes that, 'He was a charismatic in the sense that he manifested a **power** and **authority** which was not his own, which he had neither achieved nor conjured up, but which was given him, his by virtue of the Spirit-power of God upon him.'[40]

The heart of living by the Spirit is to walk in the anointing God gives us – to walk in his presence and power. Acts 10:38 declares,

> '*God anointed Jesus of Nazareth with the Holy Spirit and
> with power, who went about doing good and healing all who
> were oppressed by the devil, for God was with Him.*'
>   (NKJV emphasis added)

An anointing is 'a supernatural enablement, grace, manifested presence of the Holy Spirit operating upon or through
an individual or corporate group to produce the works of
Jesus.'[41] But we must first 'grow' out of control.'

Growing Out of Control

Many church pastors and people are trained 'controllers.'
We are more competent in the ministry than we are in the
miraculous. We rely on good Bible teaching and preaching,
theology, counseling, church programs, and church growth
methods. We ask God to bless our programs more than we
ask Him to reveal His plans. We may even welcome renewal
but when we get the ball, we either fumble it or kick it – we
don't know what to do when we get it. We are insecure with
the supernatural. As victims of an anti-supernatural,
'enlightenment' scientific world-view, we are taught to value
control and order. Don Williams represents many of us
when he writes:

> 'In my "enlightenment" theological education, I was
> trained to control everything. Paul's dictum to do all
> things "decently and in order" is lived out by us
> Presbyterians to a fault. Thus, I was given exegetical
> tools with which to manage the Bible, theological tools
> with which to manage the faith, homiletical tools with
> which to manage my sermons, psychological and socio-
> logical tools with which to manage people and business
> tools with which to manage the church. Today's
> seminary curriculum is far advanced in the application
> of the scientific method to the professional clergy.'[42]

Does this sound familiar? Samuel Chadwick warned that
'A ministry that is college-trained but not Spirit-filled works
no miracles.' But, perhaps we have too much at stake. We
fear failure. We are insecure with the consequences. We tend

to focus on control rather than order. M. Scott Peck observes that 'The need for control – to ensure the desired outcome – is at least partially rooted in the fear of failure.' [43] We feel that success means we must conquer 'chaos.'

Margaret Wheatley, a secular business consultant, applies quantum theories to organizational management. She shows that at the quantum level there is an unpredictable chaos within order. There's order within disorder and disorder within order – that disorder can be a source of order and creativity. Space is the basic ingredient of the universe. Did you know that atoms are 99.999 percent empty?

There are also invisible 'fields' like gravity, which occupy space. [44] Now imagine the Holy Spirit who inhabits the space and literal fields in a church. Like a magnetic force, He pulls all behavior toward a common life causing ordered chaos that we can't 'control.'

Though she wrongly looks more to evolution than to God, Wheatley rightly acknowledges that life at every level is inherently orderly. It seeks organization and order. But the process is exploratory and messy. How life becomes orderly violates all our rules of good process. It is not neat, logical, or elegant. Life seeks order in a disorderly way and almost always, what begins in randomness ends in stability, because new relationships create new capacities and self-organization. Structures emerge and recede as needed in **relationships**. They are not imposed. [45] Life longs for stability in freedom not in conformity and control. She challenges,

> 'Stability is found in freedom – not in conformity and compliance. We may have thought that our organization's survival was guaranteed by finding the right form and insisting that everyone fit into it. But sameness is not stability. It is individual freedom that creates stable systems ... But then we take this vital passion and institutionalize it. We create an organization. The people who loved the purpose grow to disdain the institution that was created to fulfill it. Passion mutates into procedures, into rules and roles. Instead of purpose, we focus on policies. Instead of being free to create, we

impose constraints that squeeze the life out of us. The organization no longer lives. We see its bloated form and resent it for what is stops us from doing.'[46]

She then asks the pressing question we all would ask, 'How do we create organizations [and churches] that stay alive?' Her provocative answer:

'We need to trust that we are self-organizing, and we need to create the conditions in which self-organization can flourish. We need to become intrigued by how we create a clear and coherent identity, a self we can organize around ... Identity includes such dimensions as history, values, actions, core beliefs, competencies, principles, purpose, mission ... Every organization is an identity in motion ... We must engage one another in exploring our purpose, why we have come together ... What are we trying to be? What's possible now? ... Identity is an unmistakable and certain call.'[47]

As revived churches, let's establish our identity – our call, purpose and passion. Let's self-organize in relationships that fulfill that identity. Let's emerge together. 'We can never go back. Life is on a one-way street to novelty. It always surprises us ... Emergence is the surprising capacity we discover only when we join together. They do not exist in the individuals who compose the system.'[48] We must be present, open, vigilant, and alert to surprises. 'We need to notice things we weren't looking for, things we didn't know would be important, influences we hadn't thought of, behaviors we couldn't predict. An emergent world welcomes us in as participants and surprises us with discovery – the first step to realizing everything is a gift.'[49]

Let's co-operate rather than compete with God's quantum designs of a disorderly ordered emerging universe. Spirit life is unstoppable as it produces behaviors, relationships and structures that we can't control or regulate. Our basis must be in **trusting** relationships that enable our churches to be open and secure. Let's endeavor to **contain** the fire of the Spirit not **control** or **condemn** it. Paul exhorts, *'Do not put out the Spirit's fire'* (1 Thessalonians 5:19). Let's be willing to discard old wineskins as we open ourselves to new wine. Let's build free and flexible fireplaces that will house the flame. Freedom brings order while control brings bondage. I love James Ryle's description of freedom – 'Nothing to fear, nothing to prove, nothing to hide, nothing to lose.' From sea to shining sea, instead of control, let freedom ring with expectancy.

Expectancy

Bishop David and Mary Pytches from Chorleywood, England were at our church teaching at our *Leadership and Church Renewal School.* When we have outside speakers we usually hold a Wednesday evening worship, teaching and ministry night that is open to our church and to the public. On this evening I didn't really feel like going. I was tired from a busy week. I thought that we would have a pleasant worship time, a good message by David, a bit of prayer, and then I could go home by 9:30 pm or so. I didn't expect a great deal from God. But He surprised me.

I had asked David to speak on new wineskins and to give us a summary of what he saw God doing around the world in renewal. After all, I wanted the people to be open to the new ways that God was moving. Startled was I when he opened his message with the following,

> *'Forget the former things; do not dwell on the past. See, I am doing a new thing! Now it springs up; do you not perceive it? I am making a way in the desert and streams in the wasteland.'* (Isaiah 43:18–19)

I am very familiar with this passage and believe in it. In fact it is the opening passage to chapter one of my first book. I've always taught that we should not hang onto or dwell on the past but we should **expect** God to do new things. And yet it's easy to lose that exciting edge of expecting God to do something new.

Well, as David prayed 'come Holy Spirit' things started slowly. There was a sweetness in the room and yet a rather holy quiet. This was a typical renewal ministry time that I was quite familiar with. But then a 'presence' began to settle in. Waves of the Holy Spirit began to come over people. Some fell, others laughed, others shook, others sat or stood where they were. We continued to wait. David invited those forward who were experiencing something from the Lord. Probably a hundred people came up for prayer. Again he called 'come Holy Spirit.' As he did you could feel and see the intensity of the Lord's power sweep through the crowd. We began to pray through the crowd. An hour later I looked around to see the effects of a 'visitation of God.' I did not expect God to visit. But He came on David's expectancy rather than on mine. This was a good lesson for me. I must expect God to come, to move, to minister, to revive His Church. As Bishop Pytches remarks, 'When the supernatural touches the natural, unnatural things happen.'

It's difficult to build by the Spirit if we are insecure, indifferent, too cautious, have limited expectations, or don't believe that supernatural gifts of the Spirit are for today. Leaders are especially vulnerable. Again, as Pinnock remarks, 'Limited expectations dishonor God and diminish God's freedom to act ... Limited expectation results in an experiential deficit ... Openness does not mean knowing the outcome ... There are risks in any call for openness ... How tragic it would be if focusing on dangers closed us to the Spirit ... Leaders can impede renewal if they are unduly cautious ... Leaders are sometimes nervous about Spirit, which may explain why revivals usually break out in communities less hampered by office.' [50]

Counting the Cost

During this Wednesday ministry night with the Pytches' I prayed for and later talked to a lady who introduced herself to me as the wife of a pastor in a Baptist church nearby. She recounted how the Lord was doing 'strange and wonderful things' in their church. They came to several renewal conferences where the Lord touched them and a core group of about forty of their people in mighty ways. As she talked, her eyes filled with tears and her voice quivered. She struggled with the agony and ecstasy of wanting to build a revived church. They experienced profound effects of the Holy Spirit.

But she told me how they felt like they had to 'control and hide' what was happening in their lives. Yet, she felt that 'this thing is going to burst open if we don't open it up in our church.' She was talking about letting the Holy Spirit have His way in their Baptist church. Yet there was fear and insecurity about how the denomination and the district supervisor would respond. I understand what she meant. We went through this ourselves in 1987–88 and again in 1994. We still continue to deal with it from time to time.

My advice to her was not to leave the denomination to become a Vineyard, Charismatic or independent renewal church. Rather to try to stay where they were and count the cost with faith. In Jesus' hometown, Matthew records that Jesus *'did not do many miracles there because of their lack of faith'* (Matthew 13:58). As a contrast, Matthew also records the 'great faith' of the Roman Centurion and the Canaanite woman. They both (as Gentiles) exercised faith in the Lord's ability to heal. They then pressed Jesus with an expectancy for Him to act – and He did!

Build the fireplace and then fan the flame. The fireplace can be Baptist or Brethren – it doesn't matter – but the fire will be the Holy Spirit who is not bound by man-made denominations or theologies. The key is to count the cost, then watch God ignite the place. Yes, some people will leave; yes, there will be conflict and change; yes, you may lose your 'reputation and respectability.' But work with the leaders and go together on the journey. After you've counted the cost, there's one last ingredient that will get you there: **perseverance**.

Perseverance

Every Christian must persevere through failures, criticism, un-met goals and spiritual opposition. A revived church will experience raw God, raw flesh, and raw Devil. This causes all sorts of tension. Most of us can't handle raw stuff. We are concerned for decency, order, and control. We will need staying power. The key for staying power is perseverance – a long obedience in the same direction. The Greek word commonly translated as persevere or perseverance means 'to remain under.' People who persevere will hold the course during insurmountable odds and obstacles. They will 'remain under' the pressure as they work toward helping to build a revived church.

Winston Churchill said, 'The nose of the bulldog has been slanted backwards so that he can breathe without letting go.' On a leadership poster entitled *Perseverance*, I read the following:

'In the confrontation between the stream and the rock,
the stream always wins ... not through strength,
but through persistence.'

When an American Football team has the ball with fourth down and twenty yards to go for a first down, it can punt or throw a long pass. If they punt, they give the ball over to the opponent without a yardage gain. If they throw the long pass they risk giving the ball over to the opponent in its own territory, if the receiver fails to catch the ball. Perseverance says, go for the risky long pass. Victory might be just around the corner. The receiver might get a breakaway and carry the ball into the end zone for a game-winning touch down. A punt moves the ball away and is safer. But you don't gain twenty yards or touchdowns with punts. Many football games are won with long passes in the last minute of the game. Many baseball games are won in the bottom of the ninth inning. Many basketball games are won by one point in the last ten seconds. 'The game ain't over till it's over,' Yogi Berra declared. Persevere!

Summary

Ministry by the Spirit is through people whose hearts are aflame with God's presence – where there is vitality, life, and the miraculous while on the fireline. It is ministry that inquires of the Lord and balances the prophetic with the pastoral. Ministry by the Spirit means you will live by the Spirit. You will 'go for it,' you will 'grow out of control,' walk in His filling and fullness, as you count the cost with expectancy and perseverance. Whew!

Chapter 4

From Vision to Vehicle [51]

> *'The cities and mansions that people dream of are
> those in which they finally live.'*
> (Lewis Mumford)

As renewal and revival rush through our churches, there's
new vision stirred for God. Vision works with the future. We
must think a lot about the future because that's where we
will spend most of our time. As David Pytches tells it,
'Without vision the people perish and people without
the vision move to another parish!' And 'The man with the
vision met the man with the money. Afterward, the man
with the money got the vision and the man with the vision
got the money.' Oh the power of vision!

What is Vision?

What is vision? Where does it originate? Someone said
'vision is hope with a blueprint.' It's passion with a mental
picture. It's a burning 'yes' inside. It is a dream – a picture of
a preferred future. Charles Swindoll declares 'Vision is
spawned by faith, sustained by hope, sparked by imagination, and strengthened by enthusiasm.' Vision comes from
a divine–human synergy where God wills and acts in us
while we will and act for him (see Philippians 2:13).

What's your vision? Is it for street people, hospitality,
young adults, intercession, men, drama, or a coalition of
secular and sacred working together? What sends excitement

into your heart? It could be anything, even something unusual. What should you do with that burning 'yes' inside?

Stephen Covey says that 'Vision **gives us capacity to live out of our imagination instead of our memory.**'[52] That last sentence is profound for all of us. Let it grab you. Laurie Beth Jones calls people to focus more on what will be than on what is.

> 'The mind has one desire, and that is to see only one image. It therefore goes into overdrive trying to integrate the two, and it will put most of its energy toward the picture that is most often viewed. Therefore, people who focus only on "what is" will create more of "what is." People who focus mostly on "what could be" will begin to create "what could be." The tension in this process for many people is unbearable. Unwilling to handle the stress of seeing the two disparate images, they will "take down" or "turn off" the vision of the future, and thus slide back into the status quo.'[53]

Several times I have watched a video where Martin Luther King Jr gives his famous 'I have a Dream' speech to 250,000 people in Washington, D.C. in August 1963. I sit stunned and stirred. I see and feel the power of vision and passion. Over eight times I have also watched a live video musical performance of Yanni at the Herodian Theater in Athens, Greece. Each time I watch him perform in this outdoor amphitheater with the Royal Philharmonic Concert Orchestra it inflames my passion for God, excellence and teamwork. I saw him again live on his Tribute Tour in Vancouver with my family. Wow! What Martin Luther King Jr did with words and Yanni does with music I want to do in leading a revived church.

So, how do you get your ideas to implementation, from vision to vehicle? Let me offer the following seven steps:

1. Ask *Philosophy* questions

Ask yourself, 'Is our church an assembly plant for ministry vehicles? Is there a ministry philosophy that says "yes?" Or will I expect a "no?"' Does our church equip and unleash people for ministry according to Ephesians 4:11–16, or do we only offer pre-made programs that people must sign up for? Is there openness to new ideas? A tight hold on ministry snuffs out new ideas. Your flame will fizzle. People won't get wheels on their ideas if their leaders don't believe in axles. People approach me with ministry questions. Sometimes out of fun, before they speak, I will say 'the answer is yes!' 'Vision' and 'yes' make great friends. But they still need some restraints.

Unrestrained vision causes havoc. Churches must be strategic in what wars they will fight and when. They can't be all things to all people. Vision needs some restraints. Ask, 'Does my vision align with our church's vision and values?' Then ask, 'Will I carry my vision rather than load it onto someone else's back?' Don't expect the pastor or other leaders to fulfill **your** vision. Go to step two.

2. Draft a *Proposal*

Define your **purpose** and **goals**. Ask, 'What do I want to accomplish – why and how?' Develop options of how to accomplish the vision. For example, maybe there are several ways to start a men's ministry. Better to have several options for someone to evaluate than one. Most visions need revising as other factors and problems surface. Determine what resources and structures are available. Look for other models to get ideas, then meet with the right leader or pastor who can either refer you or will give you direction.

Present the proposal and share your heart. Anticipate their questions as you think through the possibilities and problems. If your vision has potential, they will refer you to the right person or might see you again. Then for two weeks, go from proposal to prayer.

3. Simmer in *Prayer*

Let the vision and proposal simmer in prayer. This is an important time for incubation unto illumination. Incubation – a noun from the verb 'to lie down' – often produces 'bright' ideas and creativity. Allow God to shape your vision and proposal. Let your imagination run wild as you ponder Ephesians 3:20:

*'Now to him who is able to do immeasurably more than all
we ask or imagine, according to his power that is at work
within us.'*

How much can we ask or imagine? God can do immeasurably more! People will 'chance' upon further ideas or solutions.

For example, one of our young leaders, Shawn Worsfold, presented a proposal to me for a young adult seeker service. After two weeks of incubation he came back with an eleven-page proposal for not only a seeker service, but also a complete young adults ministry and a new members follow-up and assimilation strategy! That young leader is now on staff two years later as our Pastor of Care-Groups and Young Adults. It all started with vision.

Whilst talking over lunch with Nick, one of our worship people, I chanced upon a vision for a three-month worship school. I shared it with our team. We let it simmer in prayer. A week later, while driving my car, the thoughts 'worship and prophecy' burst into my mind. That period of incubation produced a fuller vision for a three-month international school of worship and prophecy. It's happening. That one school idea led to another idea of three more schools offered over a two-year cycle. In each case above, incubation led to illumination. Let vision simmer in prayer and ask others to pray about it and give you their comments.

4. Enlist key *People*

Good visions usually require a good team to fulfill them. 'The bigger the dream, the bigger the team.' Communicate your proposal to others who may share a similar vision. Collective yearnings are like logs piled continuously on a campfire – they ignite each other and enlarge the blaze. Contact others with whom you have relationship and follow-up leads and referrals. Enlist key people who will support your vision and build a core team who will help organize it. Brainstorm. Pray together. Practice 'possibility and power thinking.'

Network with other departments, churches or agencies who may want to assist you. For example, the local Youth

With A Mission base agreed to partner with us on our first school by providing meals, lodging and staff. Another example is where people from our church started a society and enlisted the provincial government to help fund a low-cost housing project. As one more example, a person in our church proposed a vision for a performing arts guild, where musicians, actors, dancers, flag teams and artists would work together on productions and community outreaches. Set out to cultivate synergy and innovation. Enlist key people. They will support what they help create. Then move to step five.

5. Draft a *Plan*

Because they have no plan, many good visions end up in junkyards of what could have been. If you have a good vision, take the time and effort to draft a plan. You can't build a vehicle for vision without a blueprint. 'Begin with the end in mind.' Keep your vision in view as you work back to the beginning. What must you do, in what order, by when? Consult your key people to work through anticipated obstacles or objections and formulate structures that will support the vision.

Prepare a typed 4–6 page plan that expresses your vision strategy with goals and action plans. People need to read a plan and see it graphically. Let them write on it and give comments. Distribute the plan to those that require further input, depending on its importance (e.g. other pastors, elders, deacons, overseers, etc.). Make revisions and then draft a final plan.

6. *Present* the plan

After an initial 'yes' or 'this has real potential – let's talk again,' ask for a time to present the plan. Do this in person and in print for the person or persons who will give the final go-ahead. Encourage dialogue, questions and contributions. After the approval, meet with your core team and other stakeholders (those people who have a vested interest in or are affected by your vision) to present the plan and get their final input. If necessary, ask a pastor or a senior leader to speak for you while you present the vision in person with an abbreviated plan to the whole church. Your goal is to cultivate shared ownership that empowers and enlists people.

7. *Produce* the plan

Now's the time to get the vehicle on the road. Produce the plan and be proactive. Build the vehicle. Now drive it. Schuller says that 'Beginning is half done.' Be full of faith yet flexible knowing that your vision will likely be tested, criticized and changed as you go. There might be delays, but someone said 'God's delays do not mean God's denials.' After planning your work you must now work the plan and stick with it. Live, model, pray and communicate the vision, to evaluate at regular intervals and to record the fruit. Communicate on-going results with your stakeholders to keep the vision alive.

Vision Problems

You may think, 'This is all sounds great, but what should I do when I usually hear "no" in our church?' Or, 'I have a burning vision for this but I can't enlist anyone.' Consider several factors:

1. Perhaps your vision does not align with the current direction or vision of your church.
2. Maybe God is testing your vision with a delay that will forge a better product later.
3. Possibly your vision needs changes. Obstacles could be opportunities for improvement.
4. It could be the Enemy set an ambush to sabotage your vision.
5. Perhaps you have run into a wall of 'problem perceivers.' In *Developing the Leader Within You*, John Maxwell writes:

    'Some people can see a problem in every solution. Usually obstacles are the things you see when you take your eyes off the goal. Interestingly, some people think the ability to see problems is a mark of maturity. Not so. It's the mark of a person without a vision. These people abort great visions by presenting problems without solutions.' [54]

Your options are:
- opt for 'the death of the vision,'
- pray that God will resurrect it,
- wait for better timing,
- engage in spiritual warfare intercession,
- help problem perceivers to see beyond the problems, or revisit the process.

If you must help problem perceivers or revisit the process, go back to the same people to share your heart, paint an exciting picture and sell the problem to which your vision is an answer. Few visions score a home-run the first time at bat. You may have to wrestle for your vision as Jacob wrestled the angel for the blessing (Genesis 32). However, if you still can't get a 'yes' and believe God inspired them, look for an alternative way to fulfill it.

Putting it All Together

Trey Bourette, a former youth leader in our church, proposed a vision for a flea market that I believe the Spirit birthed. But with all Spirit-birthed visions, come testing and difficulties. He and I discussed the philosophical and practical issues. As a small business, he wanted to establish it for personal income but also to raise money for youth ministry. He asked to hold the flea market on our church parking lot on Saturdays. He would pay rent and ensure quality control. It seemed to align with our vision for creative financing, multi-use of our facility, and community involvement. I requested a written proposal. I would then take it to our leadership team and elders for dialogue. We let it simmer in prayer.

The initial process was difficult. A few felt we would turn the temple of God into a commissary of money-changers instead of a house of prayer. Others felt we would invite vandalism, theft, and the selling of offensive products. Some felt we should trust God for finances and not seek 'secular' ways to generate income. After prayer and discussion, we reluctantly decided to run the market for a year while we monitored quality control. Then we would make a final decision.

After the first year, we decided to eliminate it. It looked too 'tacky' on our property, some products were questionable and the perception that we would turn the temple of God into a den of thieves persisted. Death of a vision – or so it seemed. In the ensuing weeks, we received letters from people who appreciated the market (including some of our people and a few vendors).

The next year, our former youth pastor communicated his vision to plant a church and therefore left our staff. Simultaneously, we were facing financial difficulty. We'd have to recruit more volunteers and reduce expenses. Trey Bourette, who proposed the flea market, had also worked with our youth for eighteen months and by clear affirmation was the best pick as a successor – but we could not pay him. He then proposed a revised vision. He wanted to fund himself as a youth pastor through the profits that he could make from the flea market on Saturdays. If we gave him free rent, he would not draw a salary from the church. Furthermore, he still wanted to generate funds for youth ministry and to involve youth in the market as a community outreach. He gathered reference letters from vendors showing the effect that he'd on their lives and morals the previous summer. He also reported on fruitful contacts made through 'servant evangelism,' praying for people, and building relationship with vendors.

I asked him to enlist key people and to draft a new plan for distribution to the pastoral team and elders. He would then come to an elder's meeting to present his plan in person. The meeting produced synergy and innovation as he shared his heart and helped us look beyond the obstacles. Together we discussed how this was a creative way to release a 'tent-making' youth leader with a community impact result on our turf. Furthermore, the market had no correct parallel to the money-changers in the temple as we weren't embezzling money from our worshippers. We decided to call it an 'open-air market' to remove sultry connotations, to try the idea for one more year and to have him share the vision at our annual meeting and on Sunday morning. We distributed forms to our people asking for feedback. Ninety-eight percent of those who filled out the forms were for it. Two months later he produced the plan.

He ran the market for two years and funded himself through it but also with partial help from the church. All the while he also developed a recycling company and became the key visionary for our annual Student Revival Youth Avalanche Conference. As a result, thousands of youth have come to get 'Sold Out' for Jesus as they experience renewal and revival with revenues enough to fund our new youth pastor. Trey has now left to pursue his vision to be a youth missionary in the Northwest and to develop regional Youth Avalanche conferences in strategic cities in the Western US and Canada. He has a vision for youth revival. It all began with a vision for a flea market to fulfill his vision for a self-funded youth ministry in our church.

To achieve what Steven Covey would describe as a 'Win\Win' situation (a deal in which both parties benefit equally), is a worthy goal. But for all to win, we must own a common vision. 'Without it,' John Maxwell writes, 'energy ebbs low, deadlines are missed, personal agendas begin to surface, production falls, and people scatter.' Helen Keller was asked, 'What would be worse than being born blind?' She replied, 'To have sight without vision.' As you contribute your part in helping to build a revived church, may God empower you and enable you to get wheels on your ideas for ministry as you go from vision to vehicle,

> *'For it is God who is at work within you, giving you the will and the power to achieve his purpose.'*

> (Philippians 2:13,
> Phillips)

Chapter 5

Going for Renewal Toward Revival

Answering the question, 'How do you have a revival?'
British evangelist Gipsy Smith replied, 'Kneel down and
with a piece of chalk draw a complete circle all around you.
And pray to God to send revival on everything
inside the circle. Stay there until He answers,
and you will have revival.'

Our church experienced a mind-bending, heart-touching outpouring of the Holy Spirit in late 1987–88. The Holy Spirit came with power again in the Spring of 1994. When the so-called 'Toronto Blessing' hit the Airport Vineyard Church, we had already seen thousands of hours of that expression of renewal in our church. We logged time in prayer meetings and then in conflict management meetings as we tried to administrate new-found prophecy, words of knowledge, dreams and visions, power encounters with demons, and astonishing manifestations. We were truly surprised by the power of the Spirit!

With all the good, the bad, and the ugly, I've learned that it's unwise to invite the Holy Spirit to 'come,' and then after He does, to stand back and just say 'more.' Intelligent God-fearing people have serious questions we must answer. Some God mixed with some flesh and/or the demonic can cause havoc. Or lots of God **not** mixed with flesh or the demonic can also cause havoc.

Even as Rush Limbaugh believes that the majority of Americans hold traditional values and are conservative at heart, I believe the same about Christians. People need the

prophetic to encourage and exhort them. They also need the **pastoral** to care for and caution them. All people need care, love, safety and security. They need churches that are relevant and safe enough to bring un-churched friends and family to. They need pastors who preach the Bible along with strong Sunday schools and youth programs. People really want God. We cannot build or sustain a church on renewal alone. However, we can cultivate a common vision for genuine revival.

Organize Around a Common Vision

Revived churches will see themselves as a part of a larger global movement that embraces and experiences revival. As David Bryant remarks, 'The most strategic thing revival-minded Christians can do is to grow as advocates of revival before God and before others and to mobilize others with them into a movement of seekers determined to settle for nothing less.'[55]

Get with your pastors, leaders and other interested people. Develop a common vision for a revived church. Bryant suggests the following strategy:

1. **Embrace the vision**. Bring others into the hope of spiritual awakening.
2. **Build the vision**. Read about revivals, develop a biblical foundation for revival, seek out communication networks that will keep you informed of broader developments in revival and seek out 'pools of renewal' in churches and organizations.
3. **Integrate the vision**. Actively integrate your vision for revival into everything else you do in following Christ.
4. **Share the vision**. Enter into relationship with a team of people who encourage each other and strategize together on how to more effectively mobilize people toward revival.[56]

From Renewal to Revival

I offer the following paragraphs, expanded from my first book *Let the River Flow*,[57] to help you answer the question,

'How can I help my church go from renewal toward revival?' We must be careful to not formulate external laws which we hope will serve as formulas for success. My purpose is to not give laws and methods, but rather to point to a path of disciplined grace. The path of the revived church is like the path that Richard Foster outlines for spiritual growth. In his book *Celebration of Discipline*, he makes a vital point, 'We must always remember that the path does not produce the change; it only places us where the change can occur. This is the path of disciplined grace.'[58] Revived churches begin with revived people.

1. Learn the biblical, historical and current experiences regarding renewal and revival. Through the years we have taught on the subject of renewal and manifestations – much of what I wrote in my first book and what I write in this book we have taught our people. In 1994 we did an entire series especially for all the newcomers on the current renewal from a biblical, historical and contemporary perspective. Based on Gordon Fee's book, *Paul, the Spirit, and the People of God*, in late 1997 we did a series on 'Being The People of the Presence' followed by one on 'Revival.'

2. Overcome fear and wrong perceptions. Share personal testimonies that demonstrate the fruit. Request forums and meetings where you can ask questions and where non-defensive dialogue can occur. Be involved in worship, prayer, serving and intercession. Also, attend good conferences, and learn from useful books, tapes and videos. Don't push your pastors or other people. Be gracious and not argumentative or defensive.

3. Work with your key leaders and those being touched in significant ways. It's difficult for two to walk together unless they are in agreement. Therefore, it is important to consolidate your heart and vision regarding revival with your leaders. Leaders are influencers. If they buy in, most of the way will be paved. It they do not buy in you will have a very rocky road. I know many pastors who have lost their churches because of leadership conflicts over renewal and revival. When pastors and people share renewal experiences together, it can cultivate a common vision. When pastors or people have these experiences on their own and try to bring it back into their churches, alienation often occurs.

4. Seek after and emphasize the fruit. Do not judge the whole by the part. Most people work and perceive at the micro-level (the small picture, the details). Leaders must work and perceive at the macro-level (the large picture, the generalities). If we emphasize and look for fruit, and observe the whole rather than the parts, we will build more effectively.

5. Be willing to take risks – 'No pain no gain.' To go for renewal toward revival requires faith and risk-taking. However, sometimes you may be caught off guard with people or situations that can needlessly alienate the unsaved or the uninitiated. To be reckless is unwise. There is an element of being 'seeker-sensitive' as Paul seems to argue in 1 Corinthians 14. Be **in control** without being **controlling**. For example, we held a 'Healing and Revival' conference at our church. On Sunday morning we had a usual service. We invited one of the conference speakers to preach and minister. He caught us off guard with some of his teachings and style but God displayed his power through him at a remarkable level. It did offend many.

During the ministry time, things almost got out of control. There was quite a spillover from the conference with strong, loud physical and emotional manifestations. Our people have seen a lot, but this was almost too much for some – especially visitors and the unsaved. We talked to several of our leaders and issued a letter to the church the following Sunday to express our pastoral concerns. After we issued the letter and had talked to many, you could tell that people felt relieved that we were 'in control.' Tom Landry, the Dallas Cowboys head coach, understood this when he said, 'Leadership is a matter of having people look at you and gain confidence, seeing how you react. If you're in control, they're in control.'

6. Continue to value the whole Bible with Christ at the center. Spurgeon said, 'A Bible that is falling apart usually belongs to someone who isn't.' The tendency is to jettison the Bible and want the Spirit at the center. But the Spirit's ministry is to glorify Christ (John 16). Place a high value on the Bible and all in-house ministries. While it's easy to discard the more 'mundane' things of church life, don't fall prey to this temptation. Some people would like to commit themselves primarily to renewal meetings. John Wimber warns, 'When you made that choice, you gave up your church. You'll not end up with a church. You'll end up with a 'revival' center full of strangers that have had a common experience. In seeking something that is good, be careful not to sacrifice the best.' We must work for obedience to God, not just fascination with God. Eugene Peterson sounds a warning: 'It is easier to pursue a fascination with the supernatural than to enter into the service of God. And because it is easier, it happens more often. We have recurrent epidemics of infatuation with religion. People love being entertained by miracles.'

7. Get immersed in but go beyond renewal. You still live in a very real world of frustration, pain and stress. You still have a family, a job, a ministry and personal problems. Renewal will not replace the need for small groups, children's and youth ministries, good Sunday morning services and so on. Renewal will certainly improve things, but it cannot be a substitute. Some people say, 'Well, we've experienced renewal for the past six months now and things seem to be dying out. We can only preach to and pray for ourselves for so long. Is something wrong? What shall we do?' My reply is this: there comes a point when the church is renewed! If you hold renewal meetings and don't keep adding new wood to the fire with new people coming in, the old wood is burned up and the fire begins to subside. This is natural and not bad, as you cannot sustain an indefinite renewal.

After you are renewed and filled by the Spirit, make contact in your spheres of influence as a witness in mission, mercy ministry, evangelism, the multiplication of cell groups, church planting, community service, and so on. Go out and do good to people. Buy someone a hamburger. Pray for a sick neighbor. Go on a missions trip to help build an orphanage in Mexico. If we only contain the waters of renewal, we will become like the Dead Sea. It has the fresh waters of the Jordan River flowing into it, but without an outlet. Thus the Dead Sea becomes a dead reservoir of water. We must be channels and not containers of God's blessing. Yes, we need to build fireplaces to contain the fire of God, but we cannot keep it there to only warm ourselves.

8. Be prepared for resistance, criticism, opposition and 'the cost.' Whenever the manifest presence of God comes, there's fall-out. Jonathan Edwards said: 'There never yet was any great manifestation that God made of Himself to the world, without many difficulties attending to it.'

9. Express your emotions. Crying and laughing are the two most common emotions – why? Because there are so many hurting people that have so much pain and bottled-up frustrations. When God is present, you might cry. When the Holy Spirit touches people at their deepest levels, intense weeping and rejoicing often result. Western Christians are taught to be intellectual and not emotional.

During times of intimate worship or passionate preaching, people also become emotional. After all, are not worship and the Word of God to be full of wonder? Have a look at the book of Psalms – a very emotional collection of faith-filled praises and prayers. Empowered evangelicals are taught to love God with all their minds but what about all their hearts? Even Billy Graham understood this when he said, 'Some people accuse us of too much emotionalism. I say we have too little. That is why we are losing church people to other interests. We need not only to capture their minds; we've got to touch their hearts. We've got to make people feel their faith.'

10. Don't model or promote an anti-intellectual spirit. Don't model or promote hastily given prophecy and 'words.' Prophecy must follow the New Testament guidelines with wisdom and patience. Don't become a prophecy, dreams, visions, manifestations and experience 'junkie.' Do not throw out your mind and common-sense wisdom. Granted, many evangelicals have more Bible in their heads than Spirit in their experience. Don't announce 'healings' before the facts are thoroughly verified. Don't model or promote unrestrained 'enthusiasm' and so-called 'abandonment.' Don't judge the work by the intensity of manifestations, zeal or joy. There's a vast difference between promoting freedom in the power of the Spirit, biblically governed, and careless emotion-driven euphoria. Internal fruit rather than an external show is the goal. Jonathan Edwards warns of this concerning the revival in Northampton in 1740–42,

> 'The **effects** and **consequences** of things among us plainly show the following things, viz. That the degree of **grace** is by no means to be judged of by the degree of **joy**, or the degree of zeal; and that indeed we cannot at all determine by these things who are gracious and who are not; and that it is not the **degree** of religious affections but the **nature** of them that is chiefly to be looked at. **Some** that have had very great raptures of joy, and have been extraordinarily filled, and have had their bodies overcome, and that very often, have manifested far less of the temper of Christians in their conduct since than some others that have been still and have made no great outward show.'[59]

11. Embrace repentance and unity. Dr Michael Brown, of the Brownsville Assembly of God Church, asserts that the depth of revival will correspond to the depth of repentance in the hearts and lives of people. We must welcome holiness of conduct and character, in actions and attitudes, in our public and private lives. This is an act of humility. Someone has said that 'No humility, no health, no repentance, no humility.' No revival has come without prayer and repentance about the sin in our lives. To repent means to turn or return and to change one's mind and therefore change one's behavior from sin to God.

In late March 1998, about two-thirds of our way through a 40-day season of fasting and prayer during Lent, I held a meeting with our pastors, elders, deacons, and their wives. Our purpose was to discuss the current place of our church, to communicate what God was doing and where we were going, and to pray together. The Spirit began to move in our midst and to lead us into confession and unity. As we began to pray, the group, through prophetic discernment, was exhorted to stand in the gap and intercede for people they represented in our church – people with fear, with critical spirits, with complacency, with hope deferred, with control

issues, and so on. Two Scriptures that came out were
Ephesians 4:3, *'Make every effort to keep the unity of the Spirit
through the bond of peace'* and Psalm 133:1, *'How good and
pleasant it is when brothers live together in unity!'*

Over half the group began to repent of attitudes and
actions in their own lives that also represented others in
our church. With tears of repentance God began to restore
unity among us leaders of the church. At the very end, one
of our elder's wives, Rena Cole, said, 'I feel silly but I feel like
there's a fire in the middle of the room.' She got up and ran
there. While standing there she began to tremble under
God's power. Soon the whole group got there with her. As
we began to pray for one another the fire spread. People
began to fall under the power, the prophetic and laughter
started to flow. There was an electric presence of God with
the spirit of unity present – a foretaste from renewal toward
revival.

12. Be active in prayer, embrace humility and let God be
God. The unleashed power of God will come through
humble people of prayer. 'You cannot read far into the story
of a revival,' declares Brian Edwards, 'without discovering
that not only is prayer a part of the inevitable result of and
outpouring of the Spirit, but, from a human standpoint, it is
also the single most significant cause ... Prayer is both the
cause and the result of the coming of the Spirit in revival.' [60]
This report about a humble, praying, William Seymour in
the Pentecostal Azusa Street meetings in Los Angeles at the
turn of the century illustrates what I mean:

> 'Brother [William] Seymour generally sat behind two
> empty shoeboxes, one of top of the other. He usually
> kept his head inside the top one during the meeting, in
> prayer. There was no pride there. The services ran
> almost continuously. Seeking souls could be found
> under the power almost any hour, night and day. The
> place was never closed nor empty. The people came to
> meet God. He was always there. Hence a continuous
> meeting. The meeting did not depend on a human
> leader ... No subjects of sermons were announced
> ahead of time, and no special speakers for such and

hour. No one knew what might be coming, what God would do. All was spontaneous, ordered of the Spirit. We wanted to hear from God, through whoever He might speak. We had no "respect of persons." The rich and educated were the same as the poor and ignorant, and found a much harder death to die. We only recognized God. All were equal ... Those were Holy Ghost meetings, led of the Lord.'[61]

Chapter 6

Getting Equipped
for the Adventure

'And He Himself gave some to be apostles, some prophets,
some evangelists, and some pastors and teachers,
*for the **equipping** of the saints for the work of ministry,*
***for the edifying of the body of Christ**, till we all come to*
the unity of the faith and of the knowledge of the Son of
God, to a perfect man, to the measure of the stature
of the fullness of Christ.'
(The Apostle Paul, Ephesians 4:11–13, NKJV)

Fresh from Bible college, I ventured into my first ministry assignment as a summer interim pastor at a century old traditional Baptist church. I preached on Sundays and led a Wednesday night Bible study. At 26 years old I felt like they should call me 'sonny' rather than 'pastor.' The majority were elderly people who were very patient with me and loved God. On one Wednesday night Bible study, we got into a discussion about the role of pastors. I tried to convince them that the role of a pastor is not primarily to do the ministry but to equip the saints to do it. One of those saints, a woman who'd been a member there for over 50 years, wouldn't buy it. I directed her to Ephesians 4:11–12, waxed eloquent on the text, and sat back to await her reply. I thought, 'I've really got her now.' After we read the text she said, 'I've never heard of that before!' I didn't know if she was surprised or in denial – maybe some of both.

I wonder how many people today believe that equipping the saints for **them to do the ministry** is a primary role for church pastors? Do you know that 80–85% of all churches in North America have plateaued or are declining in numbers; that 85% of all churches average 200 or less on Sundays, or that 50% of all churches average 50–75 in Sunday attendance and don't grow beyond? Why? There are several reasons. A major one is a failure to equip people to do the ministry. You can't help build a revived church if you'd rather sit in the pew than get on the playing field. After catching the fire we must go on to construct fireplaces with people equipped for the adventure, as each one does their part (Ephesians 4:16). The word 'edify' in Ephesians 4:12 means 'to build up.' Let's get equipped for the adventure. You have a major part. In Randy Clark's words, 'God can use little 'ole me!'[62]

The Equipping Environment

We can think of equipping with methods, programs or classes for the individual. Or we can think of an environment where leaders facilitate equipping and people respond systemically throughout the church. For example, Stevens and Collins write,

> 'A pastor may facilitate a training program for lay pastoral care giving, but if the environment communicates that only a professional can be of any help, the program is undone by the environment. The problem is systemic ... A lay leader may start a discipleship training program, but if the relationships in the church are impersonal and functional, the training program is at odds with the systemic reality of the church.'[63]

If the Sunday morning environment communicates something different (i.e. that only trained and appointed leaders and pastors can minister) we might shoot ourselves in the foot even though we preach about and 'believe' in equipping. The medium is the message. We declare our values in our practices and priorities. The Sunday morning environment should help model the value of every-member ministry.

Lay-people want and should do much of what pastors do. If it's visitation and care, many lay-people are good care-givers. If it's praying for the sick or evangelizing the lost, lay-people are out in the world making contact with sick and lost people. If it's teaching or leading worship, many lay-people are gifted teachers and musicians. The church unleashed can be a place where we all get to play, not just the star players or hired professionals.

In revived churches – where there is an environment of vision and Spirit – this is especially crucial. Equipping takes on an even more environmental aspect. Prayer, care-giving, evangelism, kingdom ministry, spiritual gifts, and holy living are 'caught as much as taught.' As we observe people doing and being this stuff we begin to 'get it.' Further, as we participate ourselves, we learn it. Someone wrote, 'I heard and I forgot. I saw, and I remembered. I did, and I understood.'

Stevens and Collins further write that 'the most direct way to equip the saints for the work of the ministry is not to devise strategies for equipping individuals but to equip the church (as a system). Then the church will equip the saints.'[64] Also, 'equipping is essentially a relational, rather than a programmatic ministry; this involves building the people of God.'[65] We need to be around other people as apprentices are around journeymen to learn the crafts of the trade.

Because most churches focus their equipping on courses and content, they tend to be unaware of environmental factors. You've probably enrolled in Sunday school or training classes where the primary method for teaching was listening to a lecture or filling in a set of notes. The environment was cold and academic. The environment also involves the climate.

The Learning Climate

When the learning climate is 'hot' people can't get enough fast enough. The learning climate can become 'cold' if ineffective methods of teaching are used. While in Seminary I took many courses on great subjects – most of which I've forgotten and many of which were unrelated to life and ministry. Many were merely lectures where the professor poured from his jug into my mug. I learned tons of information. Kind of like taking a four-year course on the theory of how to play piano, getting an 'A' on the final exam but never having to play the piano itself. However, the courses that are still with me today are the ones where I was involved in the process, where I got to 'do it' and where I made connections between content and practice. The 'hot learning climate' is a central issue.

Are You in the Hot House?

A 'hot learning climate' begins when we are Spirit-led into an awareness of what we know or don't know on a subject and what is possible in that area. For example, if you believe that God raises the dead but have never seen a corpse raised, then you are unaware of how much you don't know. However, if you saw someone being raised from the dead and the teacher told you that he wanted you to pray for the next dead person a 'hot learning climate' would begin. Immediately, you would want to know everything about the process. Or, let's say you came across a person who has a demon or terminal cancer. Your teacher says, 'go pray for that person's healing.' You'd want to know everything you could about deliverance or healing. If you saw your teacher succeed, you'd have an expectation any time he or she prayed.

Getting equipped is exposing ourselves to something more than we have experienced and expanding our knowledge with new levels through experience. We can 'get equipped through exposure' writes Paul Stevens. When we expose ourselves to teachers, healers, prophets, evangelists, intercessors, and those who practice hospitality and mercy, informal equipping through modeling will occur. You will learn about riveting revival preaching if you sit through half a dozen of Stephen Hill's sermons at Pensacola's Brownsville Assembly of God Church. You would have learned about mercy if you had visited Mother Teresa for a week. Both are hot climates.

A 'hot house learning environment' is where you are exposed to a 'hot climate' over a long time. For example, this could be anything from a week-long renewal conference to an intensive training course such as YWAM's discipleship training school. Have you ever wondered why conferences are so intense, why the people sing with so much passion and why the prayer times are generally very powerful? It's because there's a faith and expectation level that produce a hot-house learning environment. A key is receiving impartations of the Spirit.

Impartations of the Spirit

To get equipped requires:
1. **Understanding** for the mind,
2. **Inspiration** for the heart,
3. **Skill** for the actions, and
4. **Impartation** for the spirit.

If we enter an environment or 'ethos' where the Spirit is free to move, and where the Bible is taught with good worship beforehand and prayer ministry following, we will often receive an **impartation** or 'imprint' of the Spirit. An impartation of the Spirit is where the Spirit bestows a share of His presence and power to a group or individual to share in His ministry. Paul expressed this to the Roman church:

> *'I long to see you so that I may impart to you some spiritual gift to make you strong.'*
>   (Romans 1:11; see also 1 Timothy 4:14)

For example, the so-called 'Toronto Blessing' is really an **impartation** of the Father's love for spiritual and emotional healing and intimacy with God. Equipping is not only for doing stuff. It is also for being someone who is more free, alive, and empowered. How do you get equipped for intimacy with God? Well, you learn about prayer and who God is and so on. But without an impartation in an environment of intimacy you mainly learn information.

Get Oriented, Involved and then Equipped

For several years we would bring our home-group lay-pastors together on a weekend to train them. We'd give them reams of great information on how to lead care-groups. Then we'd send them off to lead them. One problem – very few could effectively apply the content to leading a care-group. The result, many were no better 'trained' when they left than when they arrived. Has that ever happened to you? You took a great training class and got lots of information that inspired you while you took notes but when you got back to your dirty dishes and fighting kids you did nothing with it. That was a poor model for learning. You heard information but received little formation and impartation. You weren't equipped.

I discovered a very helpful model presented by Carl George and Robert Logan. They write, 'Training involves three different steps: **orient**, **involve**, and **equip**. The American education model tells us to **orient**, **equip**, and **involve** (in that order).'[66] Now I try to orient, involve, and equip (in that order). When you are first oriented to and involved in the ministry task, you will develop felt-needs for later teaching related to what you are experiencing. For example, you want to teach Sunday school. Better to go in there and find out what the job entails, serve for a while, begin to see what training you will need, and then come back to get the training out of felt-need.

When I was in college I took a course on marriage and family and I wasn't even married yet. It was an exciting course. I thought when I did marry I would have an advantage over all those other foolish husbands and dads and I would do it right. Well, guess what? I forgot all I 'learned' and now find myself scrambling for James Dobson books to keep me from having a breakdown. I have major felt-need now after 19 years of marriage and three children!

Get Involved in Ministry

When we first planted our church we asked every newcomer to read Frank Tillapaugh's book, *Unleashing the Church*. It is still central to our philosophy of ministry. The bottom line: we can trust people with ministry as we unleash them to be led by the Spirit to do what they are called and gifted to do. Prove yourself trustworthy and do stuff. Keep away from rear echelon boards and committees and get into front-line ministry where the action is. It's more fun to heal someone with cancer or lead someone to Christ than to sit on a committee and debate or decide how you are going to start a healing or evangelism ministry.

'Let Go and Let God'

Leaders must allow the Holy Spirit to be in control of their people whom they should trust with ministry. This requires constant acts of faith on their part. Denny Gunderson makes a good point,

> 'That which allows a leader to release people into their own ministry can be summed up in one simple word – faith. All leaders display faith in one form or another. Some place their faith in the quality of a training program. For others, it is faith in their own leadership ability. In both instances, the shallowness of faith will be exposed by the inability of the leader to trust those whom he releases ... The ability to extend trust to frail mortals displays the depth and quality of faith one has in God.' [67]

Some accuse John Arnott of letting too much disorder occur in his meetings. However, his value on 'letting go and letting God' is perhaps better than some who want to exercise more restraint and 'order.' John honestly doesn't want to quench the Spirit as he puts implicit faith in the Spirit's work in and through people. As we gain experience we will increase in our anointing and authority. This is similar to David's relationship with Jonathan and Paul's with Barnabas. We can trust God's faithfulness. Gunderson states that,

> 'There are times when God calls us to decrease in order to elevate others. Making this choice requires an implicit trust in God's faithfulness. We must acknow- ledge that He is the One who ultimately controls our destinies ... One of the deepest fears in the human psyche, particularly for leaders, is the fear of not being

in control. Such a fear stands in stark contrast to one of the basic principles of servant leadership. The servant leader is one who chooses to decrease by willingly laying aside his own ego in order to champion the ministry of others.' [68]

You see, this is all part of the equipping environment that I wrote about earlier. As leaders trust people with ministry and let go, God is faithful to gift them and use them. Perhaps you lead a department, a training class, a Bible study or a small-group. Look around at whom you can recruit to do some of the teaching, praying or helping. Don't do it all yourself. All the while, get further equipped for the adventure. Below are some ways to do so.

Types of Equipping Environments

You learn best as you see, hear, smell, taste and do. Isn't it great to give a 'bang on' word of knowledge or personal prophecy or to worship God so gloriously that tears fill your eyes and your hair stands on end? You could study a book on prophecy or attend a seminar on worship but that's like looking at one of those realistic-looking, but fake meals in the display case at a Japanese restaurant. You want to eat the real thing not just read about it in the menu or look at it in the lobby. Getting equipped to do the ministry in a hot-house environment is like eating the real meal! You get to do the stuff. Here are some ways.

Clinics

John Wimber's Vineyard training conferences were very effective for the evangelical. After each teaching session there was a 'clinic' where people could practice the 'five-fold healing model' in praying for others. Or they would wait on God to hear His voice in words of knowledge or prophecy, or be filled by the Spirit and then released to do servant evangelism. Try to practice what you are learning with first-hand application and exposure. After there is 'show and tell' go do it! If you take a course on intercession, you should intercede. If you study evangelism, go out and share your faith. If you are learning about hearing God's voice, take time to listen.

At conferences, sometimes I feel the Lord prompt me to pray for arms to be lengthened and demonstrate what I am to delegate. In one situation, I called people forward who had back, arm and shoulder problems and had them stretch out their arms to see if one was shorter than the other. I took the three worst cases where there was about a two inch difference in length. I prayed for a lady. In thirty seconds her left arm grew to the same length as the right arm – right before our eyes! For the next person, I called for a volunteer who came forward and also prayed. It began to happen even before this person prayed. The audience sat in stunned but excited silence. For the third person, I called for a youth who was 16 years old or younger to come and pray. A 16-year-old boy came forward. As he prayed, you could see the person's arm lengthen.

The next day, I asked for testimonies. Well, the 16-year-old got up and said how he thought that maybe some day when he is older he would get to pray for healing and see God's power work. But when he heard me ask for a young person to come forward, he thought, 'I'm going for it.' This equipping environment boosted his faith and gave him a first hand experience. I did it first, he watched, then he did it and I watched. I doubt he will ever forget that! It was hot!

Care-Groups

Care-groups are an excellent real-life equipping environment with the safety of friends. I can think of no better place where people can study the Bible, worship, pray for others, exercise their spiritual gifts and do outreach together. However, the leaders must release their people to do ministry and come alongside them in a coaching capacity. Care-groups must agree to allow each member to contribute something to the group and not let the leader do all the stuff. One person might be a musician. Perhaps he or should could lead the worship. Another might be into hospitality. Let them host the group. Yet another might have a passion for prayer, let them run the prayer time. A care-group can move along very nicely with a strong leader who leads worship, teaches, and prays and then encourages others to do likewise. However, because of his excellence and readiness to do it all, some of the group members are intimidated and others are simply too lazy to try.

Paul Stevens says that one key in releasing others is to cultivate a certain amount of 'planned unavailability.' If we are always ready to do it ourselves or to step in, some birds never 'leave the nest.' We must be willing to let people fail but the learning will be more effective. I basically learned how to pray for people in a small-group as I watched experienced others do it, listened to what they prayed or didn't pray, and then gradually struck out on my own. When the Spirit is present and relationships are safe, a hot-house learning environment will occur.

Conferences

Conferences are concentrated times where people arrive with great expectancy for worship, teaching and prayer ministry. The critical mass mingled with faith provides an effective fireplace for equipping. Most conferences have main sessions and afternoon workshops where people experience different levels of information and impartation. There are many conferences out there today. I would select the ones that hold the best promise of a hot-house learning environment. People say, 'Well you can get the tapes.' Yeah, but you rarely get the impartation or equipping.

Classrooms

Though lectures usually comprise classroom training, they can be interactive and application-oriented mingled with worship, prayer, the prophetic, clinics, and outreaches. My philosophy of teaching is 'The less you teach the more you teach.' I present about half the content that I used to because I know that people cannot learn much information in a short space of time – they become overwhelmed. Instead, I always try to relate a few main ideas to real life, invite interaction, and point them toward specific application. I also try to balance Spirit and spontaneity in a hot-house climate together with structure and organization.

For example, I was teaching a course on building a revived church. I discussed the need for a balance of structure and spontaneity. As I got up to teach after the worship, I sensed a depressed mood in the room. I knew that if I taught right away, I would face an inattentive class. Instantly, I felt a slight nudge in my spirit to begin praying for the class. As I prayed for a release of joy and blessing, the mood of the room lightened. Then I felt another slight nudge to go through the class and pray for different students. I had no idea what I would pray, but as I began the words began to flow like a river. I would pray for one until I had felt nothing left to pray. I then walked over to pray for another and then another and so on. In the end, I ministered in prayer and prophecy to about eight students who sat with tearful eyes and radiant faces. The Spirit led me by an impulse. Then I asked for responses to evaluate whether that which I prayed and prophesied was accurate. It was 100%!

My point is not to draw attention to what I did, but to give an example of a clinic where a hot-house equipping situation developed. All through the week I tried to model spontaneity and Spirit within the context of structure and content. At the end of the week I had **them** wait on God and minister to one another in prayer and the prophetic in a similar fashion. I taught them to be open to the little nudges as they developed a ministry mindset – one that asks, 'God, what do you want to do in this situation?'

Camps

A favorite equipping environment is camps or retreats. People can gather for outdoor fun, fellowship and food, mingled with teaching, worship, prayer, and relaxation. Even the conversation around the dinner table or around a crackling fire can be an informal equipping environment based on community. For example, we hold our men's and ladies retreats and breakfasts, and our lay-pastors training weekends at Green Bay Bible Camp. This retreat-style camp sits along the shores of our beautiful Okanagan Lake. We try to equip the heart as much as the head so that people will feel empowered and know how to do the stuff.

Coming Alongside

We need to use Christ's on the job equipping methods. 'But,' as Wimber writes, 'Christ's method of training is difficult for Western Christians to understand. There are several reasons for this. Evangelicals emphasize accumulating knowledge about God through Bible study. Christ was more action-oriented; His disciples learned by doing as He did.'[69] It was through a rabbinical model where a rabbi would minister while his disciples watched. Then they would minister with the rabbi while he watched. Then they would be sent out to minister and report back to their master. After a time, the rabbi would release his disciples who were formed in his way of life to become rabbis themselves and teach others the same way. Wimber illustrates the model this way:

> 'In the early years of my upbringing I often visited a horse farm in Illinois where my grandfather worked. He trained Tennessee walking horses. Tennessee walkers have a remarkable high-strutting gait, different from any other horse in the world. One day I was with him while he worked on a horse with a problem gait. His solution was to hitch a pacer – a horse with a correct gait – to the horse with the problem and let them walk together. After a few days, the problem horse's gait became consistent, just like the pacer's. My grandfather explained that when a horse cannot do its job, if you connect it to one that can, soon both do the job correctly. I have learned that the secret for success with people is the same as with horses: hitch a person who cannot do a job with one who can, and soon both will know how. This is how Christ trained the Twelve...'[70]

For three years, the disciples were joined to Christ in the school of discipleship. They learned the 'gait' of kingdom ministry. He came alongside them and did the ministry; let them do the ministry with Him, and then sent them to do the ministry themselves. Let's join teachers and learners. Let's come alongside people. Let's hitch ourselves with other people doing ministry as Tennessee walkers to get equipped to do our part in supporting a revived church.

Chapter 7

Blessing Our Kids and Youth

'What's done to children, they will do to society.'
(Karl Menninger)

'Youth ministry can be summed up in five words.
Love God and love youth. Period.'
(Richard Crisco,
Youth Pastor, Brownsville Assembly of God)

I'll never forget the scene. In March 1994 we held a three-day dedication celebration for our newly acquired church building. We designed the whole weekend for families as we worshipped, enjoyed activities, heard messages, and prayed for one another – adults, kids and youth together. God showed up big time! The power was so intense it was scary. On the last night God pulled out all the stops. We called the children forward. As we prayed for them the glory fell. Up until that night, I'd not seen children fall under the power of God or shake like rag dolls. Dozens of our kids were piled on the stage weeping, laughing, shaking, or lying in trances. It blew my mind. I saw five- to twelve-year-old boys and girls and our teenagers getting absolutely blasted by the Holy Spirit. I thought to myself, 'Renewal is for kids and youth too.' But they also have to get beyond the blessing. Just like adults, they need to experience God's presence and become His fully devoted followers. A revived church includes our kids and youth. Wouldn't you agree?

A Revived Church with Revived Kids

We've all struggled with the question, 'What do we do with the kids?' We want church to be meaningful for them. It's especially tough when they're small and find church boring or over their heads. They start to fidget while parents start to fume. The tendency is to send them out to Sunday School and nursery so we can worship or hear the message without distraction. Maybe you feel like the parent who was asked, 'What do you want your next child to be?' The reply: 'A grandchild.'

The problem is highlighted by the unprecedented phenomenon of peer-orientation that this generation experiences. Our children are becoming more difficult to parent and teach because they are attaching themselves to their peers instead of their parents, extended families, and teachers. Peers act as their compass or North Pole, where they get their bearings and orientation for identity, values, attitudes, and actions. God designed kids to be instinctively attached to adults. When they become attached more to their peers, adults lose their power to influence them. Parents and churches of tomorrow must **re-claim** and empower their kids today. I don't have all the answers, but let me share a few principles that might help with the process.

Bless Them

The first place to start is to bless them through emotional and physical contact – a basic attachment relationship. Notice Jesus the greatest Children's Pastor and Sunday school teacher of all time. People were bringing little children to Jesus to have Him touch them, but the disciples rebuked them. When Jesus saw this, He was indignant. He said to them,

> ' "Let the little children come to me, and do not hinder them, for the kingdom of God belongs to such as these. I tell you the truth, anyone who will not receive the kingdom of God like a little child will never enter it." And he took the children in his arms, put his hands on them and blessed them.'
>
> (Mark 10:13–16)

I know this passage is **familiar** to you. But is it **real** to you? You can do this. You don't necessarily have to 'put time' in Sunday school or children's church to bless kids. You should do that if you have the gifts and passion for it, but to make simple eye contact or a gentle pat on the back goes a long way. Talking to kids or praying for them goes even further. Show them by your warmth that you're for them. Show interest in their worlds. Why? Because 'kids are confused – half the adults tell them to find themselves. The other half tell them to get lost.'

To bless means to bestow or wish God's goodness and favor upon someone. Oh, how kids need adults to bless them! Especially when so many come from single parent homes. The church can work together systemically to bless each other's kids. Try it next time you are at church and observe how you can put an instant gleam in their eyes and a smile on their faces. The 21st century church will be a church that provides a **fathering environment** for this 'fatherless generation.' The 'spirit of Elijah' will empower the church to *'turn the hearts of the fathers to their children, and the hearts of the children to their fathers'* (Malachi 4:6). It will 'call forth' the children to be who they are meant to be and do what they are meant to do, as it blesses and includes them in the 'Father's House.' Hey, we have Mother's Day and Father's Day. What about Kid's Day? Let's bless them on a special day!

Include Them

Ruth Smelter declared, 'Every child has a right to be both well fed and well led.' We lead best when we include them in what we're doing. They absorb what they see and hear. It takes an intentional mindset to say, 'Hey, how can we include the kids in the life and ministry of the church right alongside adults?' Some of our kids have served on worship teams, have helped with our worship music overheads, as ushers, for special music, in the nursery, bookstore, and in the younger classes as Sunday school teachers or assistants. We are also strategizing ways to include children into the morning services along with the adults. Church is for the whole family.

During our first 40 day fast and prayer in 1997, we had dozens of kids participate in various ways as well. Some fasted from sweets or TV or certain meals or types of food. Our children's pastor drew up a computer picture of a bunch of 40 grapes with a corresponding Scripture to read and pray about for each day of the fast. They were to color in one grape per day as they completed each assignment. At the end, he awarded prizes to all who completed all 40. Happily, I did it with my kids. It was a great learning time as we discussed each verse and prayed together.

Teach Them

A model we are working toward is where the teachers work with the parents and kids to help train and release them. As churches we must disciple our parents to disciple their children. We need a 'paradigm shift' as we forge a vision for the discipling of entire families rather than just offering children's ministries. Teaching starts at home. Some parents expect the church to succeed in one hour per week at placing the Bible and Christian character in their kids when they fail themselves all week. Proverbs 22:6 exhorts,

> *'Train up a child in the way he should go: and when he is old, he will not depart from it.'*

What do you teach at home? Your environment and your example teach the most. 'If a child lives with criticism, he learns to condemn. If a child lives with tolerance, he learns to be patient. If a child lives with encouragement, he learns to be confident. If a child lives with acceptance, he learns to love.' We can add to this, 'If a child lives with prayer and the Bible, he learns to pray and value God's Word.' Revived churches have revived families. We revive families by teaching our parents and children to love God and obey His Word.

Of course, we should also provide excellent teaching opportunities at church too. Kids still need to get away on their own where they can learn stuff at their level. Creativity with children is important. They like action, concrete teaching, music, fun, prizes, and food. We run Sunday school in our first service and children's church in our second. In

Sunday school we use small groups for boys and girls where they can be in a relational environment with the leader and the other kids. They pray, talk together, and study Scripture. The key is **relationship**.

A few years ago I lead an age 10–11 boys' class. I had them memorize a verse each week and they each took turns preparing a Bible message they were to present to the class. We talked and had ministry times where the Holy Spirit came or where the boys submitted prophetic revelation. We went to McDonald's for pizza and to a donut shop for donuts and hot chocolate. In that 12 weeks I made a difference. Some parents still mention it to me. Hey, why not pick an age group you can relate to and try it sometime. Kids are worth it!

Finally, over the years we've offered what we call an 'Equipping Center.' These are held on Sunday evenings and open to the whole family. While the adults enroll in six week equipping classes, the kids have their own electives as well. We've offered things like mountain bike riding for kids, clowning, outdoorsmanship, kite flying, roller-blading, kids flag and dance brigade, certified babysitting courses, and one called 'Faith Force' where boys learned about prayer and preaching. The sky is the limit.

Finally, I believe that a team approach to children's ministry is for tomorrow's churches. Where administrators, prophetics, intercessors, teachers, worship and arts people, care-givers, healers and evangelists work together to serve in children's ministries. They then work with the parents who would be called on to train and impart their particular passion and gifting to the kids. Churches must begin to abandon a strictly departmental mindset in favor of a more holistic mindset. In other words, it is the responsibility of the church and the parents to bless, involve and train our kids so they will become empowered for life and service. It is not a departmental mandate but a whole church mandate.

A Revived Church with Revived Youth

E. Pinto warned, 'A society that hates its youth has no future.' The reality is, all across the church landscape, youth ministry as we have known it is in crisis. Called 'Generation X ' or 'Baby Busters,' our youth and young adults desperately need a revived church like never before. Their 'Baby Boomer' parents were born from 1946 to 1964. From 1965 to 1984 the number of their kids born declined and went 'bust' with a whole new generation of what some call the 'the postponed generation.' They don't share the values of their Boomer parents and live contradictory lives as they awkwardly search for significance. Here are the differences between Boomers and Busters.[71]

Boomers	Busters
'Me' Generation	'We' generation
Live to work	Work to live
Enlightenment world-view	Post-modern world-view
Jay Leno	David Letterman
Institutions	Relationships
Propositional truth	Relational truth
Excellence	Authenticity
Growth	Community
Lonely	Alone
Success	Wholeness

Fifty-percent of busters are growing up with unstable marriages or in single-parent homes and blended families without good role models. Says, Dan Bennett, 'Most teenagers think that their family circle is composed of squares.' They seem to have no issues to defend or causes to join. They don't care, don't get involved, and don't commit. They search for 'family.' For Busters, family is more frequently defined as those who will love them, not those who produced them. Because they experience family aloneness more than loneliness, friends become more 'family' than parents or siblings. This is the dilemma of peer attachment. The popular TV show *Friends* says it all. Thus **community** – open, safe, inclusive relationships in which people help each other rather than compete – is the highest value of this generation.[72]

Busters don't believe in absolute truth. Everything is relative. They have the post-modern perspective of the last of three umpires. The first umpire says, 'I call 'em as they are.' The second umpire disagrees and says, 'I call 'em as I see 'em.' The third umpire disagrees and says, 'You're both wrong; they ain't nothing until I call 'em.'[73] Neither does science define reality. Reality has now become what sociologists call 'virtual reality.' Virtual reality 'is an experience that's real in effect but not in fact,'[74] – a mixture of fact and fiction. Since busters can't trust in absolute truth they will trust only in what their senses can verify. Everything **could** be true. Busters find truth in their community. When pressed with logical argument, they often respond, 'Whatever.' Truth is less essential than relationships.[75]

At the same time, Busters are looking for spiritual meaning. They are open to the supernatural, the transcendent, and the spirit. Religion and boomer tradition will not answer their questions. 'This makes them as open to Christian revival as is any generation, but it also opens them to cult activity like New Age and Eastern mysticism.'[76] They will attend large-group meetings as long as they are supported with relationships outside of them.

There's another generation of youth called 'The Bridgers.' Born from 1984 onwards, this second largest group of the population (27%) will bridge the next century. They will shape the values, economics, politics, laws, and religious dimensions of our society in the 21st century. They are growing up in a multi-racial world with diverse family backgrounds. In 1993 only 71% of Bridgers were living with both parents at home, whereas 85% of 1970 Boomers lived with both parents at home. They are the first generation raised predominantly by working parents – a fatherless, day-care, and latch-key generation.

Bridgers have few moral boundaries, vanishing gender roles and are a 'religious' group but resist any claim that one faith is superior to another. Bridgers are concerned about getting a good education, a good job, and exercising their independence. They are not a 'care-free' group but are serious and searching. Bridgers are a visual and media oriented generation and their motto could be: 'I say, therefore I am.'

They read less, have shorter attention spans, are captivated by TV and videos, have money on their minds, and are

Internet and computer activists. They have no traditional political loyalties and prefer to embrace a pragmatic 'what works now' approach. They are called the 'violent generation.'[77] They contrast with Boomers,[78]

Boomers	Bridgers
Cold War	Regional wars
Nuclear threat	Terrorist threats
Economic prosperity	Economic uncertainty
Mother's care	Day-care
'Father knows best'	Father isn't home
TV dinners	Low-fat fast food
Network TV	Cable TV
45s and 'American Bandstand'	CDs and MTV
Ma Bell	Internet
VW buses	Minivans and SUVs
Free love	Condoms
VD	AIDS
Monocultural	Multicultural

Enter a revived church. It has explosive potential to offer community, significance, and salvation to these young people. In fact, roughly 75% of people who become Christians do so by age 20.[79] Religious interest wanes with age. We can't wait until youth become adults before we reach them for Christ. Traditional youth programs are not going to cut it in the 21st century. The wineskins that worked with Boomer youth will not work with Busters and Bridgers. As Richard Crisco of Brownsville Assembly entitled his book, *It's Time: Passing Revival to the Next Generation.* Did you know that the number one fear of teens is never discovering their purpose in life? And the number one fear of parents is not passing on their values to their children? We can't only rely on youth pastors and programs to do the job. As parents, 'The best time to tackle a minor problem is before he grows up.' As Jimmy Long warns, 'Any church can determine whether or not it will survive into the twenty-first century by estimating how many young people are involved between the ages of fifteen and thirty-two … A church needs at least 20 percent of its participation in the eighteen-to-thirty-two age group, or its future may be in doubt.'[80] Systemically, we must bless and revive our youth. Here are some helps.[81]

Be Real

Our youth want us to be real. For them, truth is more experienced than preached. They need real images. If we pretend we're cool or try to dress like them or listen to their music so we can 'relate,' it won't work. Let's be who we are and let them be who they are. We should be vulnerable, honest and willing to admit mistakes. Our youth pastor invited me to teach on grace in our senior youth Sunday school a few years ago. I entered the room to face the stares of about 40 young people. I swallowed hard and thought, 'Man, what am I going to do to relate to these kids?' I felt a prompting in my heart to 'Be real, Rog, be real.' For the next hour, I took off my pastoral hat and put on a personal one. I shared parts of my testimony and also the struggles I had when I was a teen growing up in southern California during the 60s. I related it all to grace. I said some pretty personal stuff because I wanted them to know I was a **real** human being not a **religious** alien called 'pastor.' The room lightened up. I then challenged them to follow Jesus and resist the temptations of youth.

Be Rousing

Busters and Bridgers can't listen to a monologue for very long. They shirk boredom. They need action, color, sights, and sounds. They need to hear, feel, and see truth communicated through stories, drama, video, music, art and media. Youth want fun. They need energetic worship and music and are attracted to passion and energy. This generation's pulse runs fast. They are the '2000 Kids' who will run the world in the next millennium. They don't want to be entertained, but want to be encouraged. Walkman's, cyberspace, MTV, music videos, ear and nose rings and black clothes mark their interests. The Saturday night amusement youth rally won't cut it anymore. Something real and rousing will. What about a youth church like *Soul Survivor* in England? Or *Souled Out* in Illinois?

Souled Out was launched in 1994. It has a Thursday evening outreach service drawing about 200–300 youth. On Friday and Saturday nights they hold a 'Heart and Soul Café' with live music, pool, and *café latte*. On Sunday evening they have their 'Get Real' service with alternative Christian rock for serious believers wanting spiritual growth. On Tuesday nights they hold intensive Bible studies in homes for girls and guys separately.[82]

At our own four day Avalanche Youth Revival Conference in May 1997, over 1500 youth from three countries, six states, four provinces and 100 churches came to 'catch the fire.' And the fire fell! Over 200 came to Christ for salvation and rededication as hundreds packed into our worship center like sardines to worship God and get walloped by the Holy Spirit. In 1998, we hosted over 1800 youth at our Avalanche 'Sold Out' Conference. The goal was to challenge them to go deep and become sold out for Jesus, a rousing cause worth joining. Youth want Jesus.

Be Relevant

Our youth view our churches the same way we viewed our parents' churches. They are largely irrelevant. We've got to communicate to Busters that, 'We believe in you. You are significant and have something to contribute.' Youth ministries cannot be babysitting services to keep our youth off the streets. They must be relevant. We must assimilate them into our churches not just farm them out to a Friday youth night. They need some organic attachment to the larger worshipping community. Get them in the worship and prayer teams, in the Sunday schools, on the missions and mercy trips, and in your homes. Get them leading small-groups, teaching and preaching, prophesying and interceding in and outside your church. Take some youth along if you go on a missions or conference trip.

Lou Engle of Harvest Rock Church and Rock the Nations declares that 'Today's Gen X youth are the Nazarite generation – consecration and commitment with fasting and prayer.' Our youth pastor Nathan Rieger says 'They are a generation needing purpose and meaning. They need a cause to join and fight for.' Shawn Worsfold, our young adults pastor remarks, 'They are a mourning generation – always wearing black.' Busters and Bridgers have a tremendous potential to be mobilized for Jesus Christ.

Thousands of teens joined in the 'See You at the Pole' movement in high schools all across the US in September 1997. They met at their school flagpoles to intercede for their schools and their nation. A Missouri based youth organization, Rock the Nations, in 1997 launched Prayer Storm, a grassroots student prayer movement founded on a four-year strategy to mobilize teens to fast and pray through December 2000. For 1997, they inspired over 2000 youth to fast and pray one day per week and repent for the sins of the United States.

Tom Cruise stated, 'A Top Gun instructor told me that there are four occupations worthy of a man: actor, rock star, jet fighter pilot, or President of the United States.' Well Tom, I've got news for you. There's four more you didn't hear about: pastor, church planter, missionary and worship leader. As God calls scores of today's youth to one of these occupations, they will not stoop to become a king. Today, Boomers hold most of the positions and power in churches. We must make way for Busters and Bridgers to come up through the ranks to join us. They want to get involved with something meaningful. They are the next millennium's ministers.

Be Relational

Josh McDowell said, 'Rules without relationship lead to rebellion.' Dialogues work a lot better than directives. Our young people have opinions and feelings and need an environment where talking **with** them rather than talking **to** them builds relationships. The key to youth is **relationship**. They value community before cause. They value authenticity before authority. Parents and pastors sometime complain that youth are unresponsive and won't commit to anything, or make sacrifices, or serve. It's hard to motivate them or get them involved. Remember what Richard Crisco said, 'Youth ministry can be summed up in five words. Love God and love youth. Period.' It's all about being relational. Youth need our blessing, big time.

Busters and Bridgers need discipleship. Youth get into gangs, drugs and sex because they want to be loved and needed. They want to belong. Revival will not hold them but relationship in discipleship will. They need to delve into the Word and the Spirit in the context of community and care. I've seen so many young people get blasted by the Spirit but go on to live reckless and purposeless lives. They did not have strong discipling relationships.

While in Norway doing a conference I was impressed with how many youth came to the meetings. Several served on the worship and prayer teams. When the offering basket came I observed the youth toss their money inside. As I preached they listened intently. On one night, I felt the Lord prompt me to call all the pastors and leaders forward for prayer. After we called for the Spirit of God, they got hammered. Then, after about 20 minutes, I asked them to turn around and face the crowd. We then called all the youth forward to stand in front of these leaders. About a hundred came forward. I then asked the leaders to now give away what God gave them and pray for the youth. In about 10 seconds pandemonium hit. All manner of moaning, yelling, laughing, falling, and shaking crashed upon those youth. These Norwegian youth were hungry for discipleship, evangelism and revival. The sponsoring church was a revived church that blessed the youth.

Summary

Jonathan Edwards reported on a revival among children and youth in the Northampton revival in 1740–42. He wrote,

> 'By the middle of December a considerable work of God appeared among those that were very young; and the revival of religion continued to increase, so that in the spring an engagedness of spirit about the things of

religion was become very general amongst the young people and children, and religious subjects almost wholly took up their conversation when they were together.'[83]

Jonathan Edwards has said what still remains to be seen for revived churches that include our children and youth for the 21st century.

PART TWO

The Spirit:
Fanning the Flame

Chapter 8

Stoking the Fireplace

*'If you want to succeed you should strike out on new paths
rather than travel the worn paths of accepted success.'*
(John D. Rockefeller, Jr)

People ask, 'What do we do with our church? We've tasted
renewal. Where do we go from here? We pray for revival.
What should we do in our Sunday morning services? How
do we ignite our church?' Well, it's one thing to 'catch the
fire' but quite another to 'contain the fire.' It's easier to
ignite a crowd (firewood) than build a church (fireplace).
Unreleased renewal can even dishearten people. A friend
recently wrote me the following: '...I also have some
cynical feelings about renewal. But I suspect this is in part
realistic and a reaction to the ongoing hype. **There must
be more** ... sure, but maybe we need to learn to walk in
what we have.' Another friend wrote this about his son and
daughter in-law (I will call them John and Jane), 'John
and Jane are experiential burn-outs – a phenomenon I
predicted several years ago. Also, pastoral care, equipping
and encouragement are lacking in many [renewal] groups.
Experience with God may be the door for some folks, but
you cannot build a deeper spiritual life on a continual diet of
it. The Word and spiritual disciplines are also needed.
History is repeating itself.'

When we are renewed, then what? Man, keep that fire
crackling and don't burn out by always looking for more
experience. Paul says it this way:

> *'Never be lacking in zeal, but keep your spiritual fervor, serving the Lord. Be joyful in hope, patient in affliction, faithful in prayer.'* (Romans 12:11–12)

Zeal refers to a combination of haste and diligence; fervor refers to 'boiling' or 'to bubble up.' The Revised English Bible translates the same verse, *'With unflagging zeal, aglow with the Spirit, serve the Lord.'* We learn to walk in what we have as we stoke the fireplace, maintain our spiritual boiling point, and fan into flame the gift of God which is in us (2 Timothy 1:6).

Because people get enthusiastic about their new experiences with the 'Untamed God' they sometimes hastily want to 'go for it.' But sometimes they unknowingly demote basic church life to second string. I think it's unwise to convert Sunday services into renewal meetings or to gear all preaching and praying toward revival. We still have 'business as usual.' When you show up to church, don't you still want engaging worship, solid preaching, anointed prayer, effective Sunday school for your kids, and so on? What occurs on Sundays is not an elective. It's a required course. We can have optional electives by holding special meetings and conferences where we can 'pull out the stops' and go for it. But meanwhile, the key is to welcome the Spirit within the 'common' life of the church. If revival hits, we might need to cancel or revise what we're doing for a while. Meanwhile, we should find ways to stoke the fireplace where business will also be **unusual** with purpose.

Being Purpose Driven

Have you ever read Rick Warren's book *The Purpose Driven Church*? [84] If not, go for it. He's the Senior Pastor of Saddleback Valley Community Church in Orange County, California. It's a Southern Baptist, seeker-sensitive, highly evangelistic church of 15,000. The 'purpose-driven' church is another way of saying the 'vision-driven' or the 'mission-driven' church. What drives your church? What drives your ministry? Is it purpose?

For us, Warren's book was timely. Over the past couple of years we became preoccupied with local and international renewal and missions. We sent out hundreds of people on ministry trips and held numerous conferences and schools. While we have done our part to 'spread the fire' many of our people needed a new fireplace. We began to hear complaints that too much of our preaching was about revival. Though our people love renewal they also love what John Wimber calls, 'the main and plain.' The **main** things of Scripture are the **plain** things of Scripture – Bible study, equipping the saints, worship, healing, helping the poor, evangelism and discipleship, prayer, fellowship, and so on.

We realized that our people were renewed! Now we wanted to strengthen the basics of the main and plain in a context of renewal toward revival. Others began to feel that the pastors didn't have enough heart for the home-base anymore. They were unsure what our purpose was. Rick Warren helped us re-define it. We had many exciting activities but they lacked a strategic focus. Our church developed health problems. Maybe you can relate.

Church Health and Church Growth

We weren't growing and lacked basic health. Many people found the back door and left. Giving began to shrink like a balloon low on air, people started arriving late for services. They generally lacked ownership. Well, we were back to renovating our fireplace! We began to ask basic questions again. We came back to the locker-room to re-define the basics of the game. Vince Lombardy did this with the losing Green Bay Packers football team when he said, 'Gentlemen, this is a football.' We had to define what business we were in and evaluate how business was. Maybe that's what you and your leaders need to do in your church. Define what your purpose is and how you are doing.

Warren maintains that church growth is the natural result of church health. He states that:

- Churches grow **warmer** through fellowship.
- Churches grow **deeper** through discipleship.
- Churches grow **stronger** through worship.
- Churches grow **broader** through ministry.
- Churches grow **larger** through evangelism.[85]

Elsewhere he remarks that, 'Health is the result of balance. Balance occurs when you have a strategy and a structure to fulfill every one of what I believe are the five New Testament purposes for the church – worship, evangelism, fellowship, discipleship and ministry. If you don't have a strategy and a structure that intentionally balances the purposes of the church, the church tends to over-emphasize the purpose the pastor feels most passionate about.'[86] I agree with Warren, but I would also add, churches grow **mightier** through renewal and revival. We must also have strategy and structure for these. Regular visitations of the Spirit will inject exuberant life into Warren's five New Testament purposes.

Over time we forged a new vision:

> *'To be a people of the Presence, saturated with God, who obey the Great Commandment, fulfill the Great Commission, and to be His Great Church.'*

Our purpose is upward, outward, and inward.

The Western evangelical church has concentrated on the horizontal arena of planning Sunday services and offering educational programs while it runs on business principles. These are not necessarily wrong, just inadequate. Revived churches will also concentrate on the vertical arena of worship, intercession, God's empowering presence, and faith. To release God's Spirit into our churches is easier when we know why we exist and where we are going. Defining your purpose helps. It may require new wiring though.

New Wiring for More Electricity

Many of us are experts in wiring but novices in electricity. We install our programs then wonder where the power is. Sometimes it's the perennial problem of keeping our old wineskins (structures) that can't hold the new wine (Spirit). Can you think of things your church used to do or still does that is lifeless? What's wrong? Maybe God's not in it anymore! When God turns up the voltage, we need a new wiring system. So, you've tasted renewal, now what?

This might sound too simple but here goes. Do the basics well – make disciples, reach the lost, plant churches, take a loaf of bread and pot of soup to a needy family, pray for your sick neighbor, teach the Bible to your kids, get equipped for your ministry, lead a small group, have communion and baptism, and worship God. But do them in the power of the Holy Spirit with prayer and in new ways with faith and passion. Become saturated with God! Like John Wesley said, 'If you light yourself on fire for God, people will come and watch you burn!'

What do Bill Hybels and Willow Creek Community Church, Sandy Millar and Holy Trinity Brompton, Rick Warren and Saddleback Community Church, John Arnott and Toronto Airport Christian Fellowship, and John Kilpatrick and Brownsville Assembly of God, have in common? I'd say they are Spirit-empowered churches that do the basics with incredible results. They seek to develop new wiring to handle more electricity. As purpose-driven churches, they experience church renewal differently but are all creative (and controversial).

You might say, 'I believe this and I try to do this. However, what's the key to unlock the power of the Spirit into my life and ministry and in our church?' I'll suggest at least four principles:
1.   Develop a miraculous mindset.
2.   Cultivate a receptive environment.
3.   Pray with fire.
4.   Do as much as you know.
These are not comprehensive and will not guarantee home-runs but they will increase your batting average.

Develop a Miraculous Mindset

We must overcome any anti-supernatural bias when we read the Bible. Do you have an unconscious tendency to screen out the miraculous passages in the Gospels and Acts? Do you find it hard to believe God does raise the dead through Christians today and that people can be transported in the Spirit from place to place just like Philip the evangelist? John Paul Jackson, a prophetic person, told me about several occasions where the Spirit transported him from one place to another in seconds where it would have taken hours. Just last year, Noel Issacs, a pastor we know in Bhutan, prayed with his family for his father James for five hours to raise him from the dead. He told the story in our church. Hey, this stuff still happens.

How many miracles do we experience in our churches? Probably less than we want. Why? Because we don't **really** believe for them. Perhaps we consume more pills than we call out in prayers for healing. We have a world-view that distrusts feelings, the supernatural, intuition, and experience. We have confidence in university degrees, reams of information, science, and sound doctrine. But sound doctrine never healed cancer nor raised anyone from the dead! Harry Blamires states, 'There is no longer a Christian mind. It is a commonplace that the mind of modern man has been secularized. For instance, it has been deprived of any orientation towards the supernatural.'[87] Pity.

To unleash the Spirit's work into our churches we must first read the Bible differently. Let's read it not as what God **did** but what God **does**. The Gospels and Acts are chock full of them. Miracles were a **normal** part of church life. Leonard Ravenhill preached that 'The church has been subnormal for so long that when it becomes normal it looks abnormal.'

There's a big difference between believing **in** the Bible and **believing** the Bible. It will take a miraculous mind-set to say 'I choose to believe that God can work miracles through me.' Go for broke. For starters, just begin praying for as many sick people as you can and then keep track of the results. For five years C. Peter Wagner did and discovered that 25–30 percent were completely healed, 50–60 percent reported some healing, and 20 percent sensed no improvement.[88] His batting average is pretty good, eh? Go for it!

Cultivate a Receptive Environment

I live in Kelowna, a sparkling jewel in the interior of British Columbia. It's a beautiful place known for its fruit industry. We grow apples, peaches, cherries, and grapes here. Before these trees and vineyards can produce luscious fruit they must have the right environment. They must be pruned, sprayed and watered. They get lots of hot sunshine in the summer. If badgered by hail, frost or heavy rain, they falter. The environment is the set of surrounding factors that contribute to or inhibit life and growth.

People also flourish or falter in different environments. For example, if a person wanted to create a hospitable environment for their guests, they'd spray air freshener, play soft background music, offer tasty snacks and freshly brewed coffee, have proper lighting, and greet the guests at the door. If the house was messy, with no music, no coffee, too bright or too dim of lighting, and had hosts that stayed in the kitchen rather than coming to the door, people would feel uncomfortable.

The Holy Spirit needs a receptive environment, an ambiance, an 'ethos' to flourish in as well. The Bible says, *'Do not grieve the Holy Spirit'* (Ephesians 4:30) and *'Do not quench the Holy Spirit'* (1 Thesselonians 5:19, NKJV). It also says,

> *'Make every effort to keep the unity of the Spirit through the bond of peace.'* (Ephesians 4:3)

Furthermore it says,

> *'Do not get drunk on wine, which leads to debauchery. Instead, be filled with the Spirit. Speak to one another with psalms, hymns and spiritual songs. Sing and make music in your heart to the Lord.'* (Ephesians 5:18–20)

Nice ethos.

The Holy Spirit prefers an environment of worship, holiness, unity, humility and expectancy. When there is bickering, doubt and discord, legalism or license, He will likely stay home or at best arrive late or leave early. Get along with your fellow church members and be nice to your spouse. When there is waiting, openness, and diligence in seeking Him, the Holy Spirit will arrive early. Lately, we've had dozens of people including non-Christians or prodigals attend our church services. The testimony is the same – they were blown away from the worship and a 'presence' that left them in either tears or in laughter.

Paul, an Irish light-heavyweight boxer started attending our church. After one service he approached me and said with a huge smile and sparkle in his eyes, 'Today, I feel like I'm walking on a cloud. I don't understand it. This is unbelievable.' On other Sundays, I'm told of people who feel a 'presence' as soon as they walk in. Before even an 'ordinary' service is over they leave in a heap of tears and emotion feeling so touched by everything. What's that? An environment of the Holy Spirit.

God gives the Holy Spirit to those who ask (Luke 11:13), but we must cultivate the kind of an environment where He will flourish. Let us cultivate it in our small groups, in our Sunday schools, in our youth groups, and in our Sunday services. Let's wake up each morning and pray as Benny Hinn does, 'Good morning Holy Spirit!'

Pray with Fire

Over the past twelve years I've produced a lot of stuff in our church. I'm a production-oriented guy. Give me a vision and I will design a vehicle to drive it in. Give me a problem and I will form a set of goals and action plans to solve it. Give me chaos and I will organize it. Give me fire and I will build a fireplace. All good stuff. But one thing I can't produce is God's presence and power. In fact, in the last couple of years I've seen that my stuff and our church's stuff doesn't work as well anymore. I now realize that I planned lots but prayed little. But that is beginning to change. I am now more intentional about giving my 'attention to prayer and the ministry of the word' (Acts 6:4). The results are beginning to show.

In the natural, our programs can work. But without the regular fresh-fire of God's empowering presence they will become as tasteless as stale bread. We cannot program God's presence into our churches through nice management ideas. It settles in through prevailing and persistent prayer. There's no other way. The church talks too much and prays too little. Have a look at the talk and the meetings in your church. You might discover, as I have, that we think, plan, problem-solve and evaluate to the point of becoming brain-dead. Generally, we rely on our education, our minds, our money, and our abilities to pull off church life. My guess is that God is not going to bless this confidence in ourselves anymore in tomorrow's church.

He will bless prevailing, persistent prayer borne in the hearts of dependent and broken people who will pray through everything. Prayer invites God's presence. God's presence invites more prayer. We should:

> *'Pray continually.'*   (1 Thessalonians 5:17)
>
> *'Pray in the Spirit on all occasions with all kinds of prayers and requests.'*   (Ephesians 6:18)
>
> *'Always pray and not give up.'*   (Luke 18:1)

We cannot stoke the fireplace if we don't pray with fire. In the words of David Yonggi Cho, 'We must pray and then obey.' I will devote Chapter 10 to this subject.

'Do' As Much As 'Know'

I have at least 1,000 books in my personal library. I have ten years of undergraduate and graduate studies jammed in my brain, have listened to thousands of hours of tapes and have attended dozens of conferences. At 46, I have concluded that I will not live long enough to practice the amount of knowledge that I have. We all know more than we do, don't we? I remember what church consultant Carl George said to some of his church people once when they wanted him to teach a Bible course: 'I won't teach anymore Bible courses until you are prepared live up to the knowledge you already have.' We have lots of information. Let's put it into practice. Paul declared, *'Only let us live up to what we have already attained'* (Philippians 3:16). To stoke our fireplaces, let's do as much as we know.

Summary

To stoke the fireplace by incorporating renewal into our lives and churches is not an easy or always pleasing task. However, once you have 'tasted and seen that the Lord is good' you will never want to go back to merely reading about Him in the menu. You will determine to do what Don Williams determined to do several years ago. I have cited a long quotation from him to express what all of us face who want revived churches:

'Now I began the long pilgrimage of incorporating what I was learning into my life, my marriage, and the ministry of the church ... This meant learning to pray for the sick and facing the problems of those who are not overtly healed. This meant learning to rely on the Holy Spirit and his gifts, to wait for His blessing, and to give up my presumption that I can control Him. This meant giving the church back to Jesus as its effective Head. This meant the struggle to enter into a deeper prayer life of not only speaking to the Lord but listening to Him as well. This meant the challenge (still in progress) of becoming an intercessor. This meant losing members who feared the supernatural or who knew that this ministry was not for them or for today. This meant facing spiritual pride, immaturity, and the emotional excesses of some of those gifted to heal. This meant fighting competition among people about their gifts much as Paul faced in Corinth. This meant more clearly defined spiritual opposition to Satan as he attacked our more open displays of the Holy Spirit's power. This meant cultural and spiritual shifts as we entered into the use of new worship music.

This meant training a whole new group of lay leaders who wanted to do Jesus' ministry in our midst. This meant defending the unity of the church for those to whom all of this was new and scary. This meant honoring the Spirit's work in those who had no empowering experience to call upon and accepting them fully rather than making them feel like second-class Christians. This meant healing for our church and the church at large across denominational and theological lines. This meant a recovery of the history of revival to see that God has always been renewing his Church down through the generations from John Wesley to George Whitefield to

Charles Finney to D.L. Moody to those ministering today. This meant recovering the Gospels and large sections of Acts and the Letters for the ministry of the church as well as for the theology of the church. This meant also the attempt to give away to other pastors and churches what God was giving to us. This meant risks of faith in living in a more biblical worldview than my old Newtonian-social Darwinian upbringing. This meant, ultimately, getting closer to the heart of Jesus and letting my heart be broken with his upon the pain of the world.

For me, there is no going back to the safety of my old life and ministry, but I am comforted by a thought from Dietrich Bonhoeffer: to be secure in Jesus is to be radically insecure in this world. So be it! [89]

Chapter 9

Wrestling with Worship [90]

'To worship is to quicken the conscience by the holiness of God,
to feed the mind by the truth of God,
to purge the imagination by the beauty of God,
to open the heart to the love of God, and
to devote the will to the purpose of God.'
(William Temple)

One Sunday I spent most of our worship time choking back the tears as the Holy Spirit carried our church into periods of intercessory worship. On this occasion, we could feel the 'thickness' of His Presence. The worship team and our church united together in harmonious communion with the Lord. I'm telling you it was overwhelming. Our worship leader, Andrew Smith, led us through an uninterrupted series of songs woven together with free-form praise and prayer. As we began to close, we stood speechless. The Spirit of the Lord was upon us when the truth of the songs and the hymn we sang burst forth in our spirits. *'Take me away with you, into the King's chambers'* (Song of Solomon 1:4) was a longing of our hearts fulfilled. We stood in a holy place.

These 'holy places' are common to all revival movements, both past and present. The flame of worship burns bright in the heart of revived churches. Each time we experience this depth at New Life, we wonder what more could possibly follow, especially when the service still has 60 minutes to go? For us, worship has never been a prelude to the preaching – a means to an end. Worship is an end in itself – to ascribe worth to God.

Part of our mission here at New Life is **glorious worship in celebration and devotion**. This flows out of our commitment to be a people who have a holy passion and lifestyle. We must go beyond renewal worship to worship that is renewed – worship that revives the church. We must call ourselves to active worship because 'worship is a verb.'

Renewal has launched our worship into new horizons of exploration and discovery. We sing new songs with new sounds. But little do most people realize that the path to glorious worship for us has been riddled with ongoing, agonizing, wrestling matches. Numerous discussions, misunderstandings, experiments, failures, and changes, are some of the contestants we have faced. Our goal in every worship wrestling match, though, is to win! The cost, we are finding, is great. The payoff, we are also finding, is greater. As leaders we are committed to 'wrestling with worship' because we know **He is worth it**. In fact, the Anglo-Saxon term for worship means 'worthship.' To worship God means to ascribe Him worth. How can you 'wrestle with worship' to ascribe worth to God? May I share some ideas with you?

Wrestle with the Heart

At the center of glorious worship is the **heart** – the place of our innermost being where our values, attitudes and motivations live. On weekends hundreds of people come with diverse tastes, expectations, and needs – this includes our worship leaders, worship and dance teams, and sound and overhead people. With this potpourri of great people, we've faced numerous challenges about issues of the heart. For example, we wrestle with how best to lead people into the kind of worship that will bring them to the Father. We've had many discussions about whether we are trying to please everyone or not. Some like it loud, others like it not so loud; some like aggressive celebration, others like reflective contemplation; some want to abandon the preaching, others want to continue the preaching; some want only contemporary songs and no hymns, others want contemporary songs and some hymns.

The core issue, I believe – for both worship teams and worshippers – is not about form and freedom, style and substance, or about 'man-pleasing.' With worship, revived churches must recognize that the core issue is about the heart in **man-serving** and **God-pleasing**. We cannot run with every complaint, and suggestion in a frenzied, reactive drivenness to please everyone. We also cannot allow the needs and particular likes or dislikes of a few impose their way on everyone else. We must release each other and work together. We are working hard at developing shared vision for incorporating a variety of worship expressions and styles that will not alienate the majority. But we must first gain victory in the wrestling match of the heart aflame with God's Spirit.

The heart issue focuses on **humility** and **servanthood**. Both people and priests must come with this two-fold frame of reference. In Matthew 4:10 Jesus declares to Satan: *'For it is written, worship the Lord your God, and serve Him only'* (a citation and slight modification of Deuteronomy 6:13). The Greek term for 'worship' in Matthew is *proskuneo* which means 'to prostrate oneself, to kiss towards.' The Hebrew equivalent, *chawah*, means 'to bow down, and pay homage' (see Genesis 18:2; Exodus 34:8; 1 Kings 1:47; 2 Chronicles 20:18 for illustrations). The second term for 'serve' in Matthew 4:10 is *latreuo* which means 'to serve as a slave for a master, and carrying out of religious duties' (see Philippians 3:3 and Hebrews 10:2). The whole posture of worship has to do with bowing down, prostrating oneself, and servanthood. The literal action reflects a heart attitude. The heavyweight opponent in this wrestling match of true worship is **pride** – wanting my thing, scorning your thing, and sticking to only one thing. Humility and servanthood call us to **teachability** and **teamwork**.

Malcolm Petch, our Pastor of Worship and the Arts, exhorts his worship and arts people to be good Christians **first**, and artists **second**. In other words, they should serve more from who they are than from what they do. Lots has to do with good communication.

Wrestle with Communication

Marriage counselors teach that communication is a key to strong marriages. To develop intimacy in marriage requires the communication of feelings, thoughts and needs. To have an un-discussed backlog of unresolved issues hinders a relationship. The same holds true for communication especially with pastors and people, and pastors and worship leaders and teams. We are learning some hard lessons. Clear and consistent communication among these three groups of people is important. We are now becoming more intentional in building these relationships and fostering open dialogue.

Over the past several years we've gone through a number of difficult changes in worship. In the past we also faced problems in the area of sound, among some of the worship team members, problems among disenchanted church people, and philosophical problems among the pastoral leadership. We suffered losses also because of spiritual warfare.

It came to a head on a Sunday evening worship night. The night was long with very loud, aggressive, instrumental and dance excursions by the worship team. This did not connect well with several of our people – and a few of the other staff as well as myself. We discussed the evening at the next staff meeting and determined to get a handle on the direction worship seemed to be going. We also had the perception that the team was developing a subtle rebellion against the interim worship leader's authority. Some of the discussion centered on whether that night involved the flesh or the Spirit and whether the worship team was truly being sensitive to, and leading the people in worship or not.

So, I appeared at the next worship team meeting with our worship leader to talk with them. As I began to share some of my 'concerns and correctives' the room grew cold. I received blank stares. I later learned that most of the team felt devastated. As far as they knew, their hearts were fully in the Spirit worshipping the Lord with all their might. My evaluation and words cut deep as I was severely misunderstood. The inner pain and turmoil that many of these people were already experiencing became even more aggravated when I, as a pastor, came to deliver this damaging blow. In my lack of relationship with some, coupled with my weakness of wanting to fix things, I played into the enemy's hands as an instrument of law rather than grace. From that point on several began to retreat into timidity and disillusionment even though I came back two weeks later to seek forgiveness. This was the fruit of some very complicated communication problems. But this was only the beginning.

We also had difficulties with the quality and volume of the sound. We couldn't agree on what constituted more reflective type songs; we couldn't satisfy scores of church people who complained of one thing or another. Everywhere we turned there were bad feelings with barriers toward openness and evaluation. Then to top it off, one summer we held an outdoor family 'Feast of Tabernacles' campout. On the concluding night the worship took an aggressive 'God Rock' style. Some of our people went over the edge. It was too radical for them. They began to make judgements and write complaint letters. The whole worship area was wrestled to the ground by disunity.

We grew weary of the match. We thought the sound and worship people would not receive communication and they thought we as pastors were in some way 'adversaries' who got in the way of 'letting them go in worship.' Some of them thought the church people were whiners that we were trying to please. We thought sometimes they didn't listen to the hearts of the people with an attitude of humility and servanthood. Most of these issues were based on various misconceptions.

It is only through non-defensive listening and teamwork that we are now winning this match. Through some very intentional meetings, where we have prayed and shared our values together, we are gaining an understanding of the different perspectives. It really shows now in the worship. We fight for unity as we also wrestle with culture.

Wrestle with Culture

As we have already discussed, in most churches there are four primary diverse groups of people:

1. Builders (born before 1946);
2. Baby boomers (1946–1964);
3. Baby busters (1965–1984); and
4. Bridgers (1984 onwards).

We have a four-fold generation gap. Each generation has its own distinct values and needs. However, in our church the pastoral leaders and worship team people are mostly from two generations: the Baby Boomers and Busters. Thus our discussions regarding what kinds of songs and worship styles are 'traditional' or 'contemporary' or 'relevant' or 'not relevant' all depends on which generation we are addressing. We all want renewal and fresh expressions of worship, but this looks differently depending on where we are, **culturally**. I received a 'paradigm shift' about this while reading Leith Anderson's book entitled *A Church for the 21st Century* (especially Chapter 8, 'What is Contemporary?'). He points out that,

> 'Traditions begin when someone does something new that others like and imitate. It has meaning ... Those who value the meaning join in the practice. When the practice is passed down to the following generation, it becomes a tradition ... Difference in the meaning of the tradition occurs because seldom does the tradition **mean** the same thing to the subsequent generation as it did to the previous generation ... To many older Christians "contemporary" means new, and they don't like it. To many younger Christians "contemporary" means new, and they do like it ... Contemporary, however, is merely a contrast to traditional. It means that it originated during this present generation rather than inherited from a previous generation. It is not better or worse; it is just later ... Contemporary is culturally defined.'[91]

The wrestling match is also with our culture. How can we be relevant while we maintain and permit those core values that mean something to each generation? The challenge is to be as inclusive as possible without losing your distinct style. Sometimes, our unspoken attitude can be 'If people don't like the worship here they can go to a different church.' This smugness will only come back to haunt us as more and more people feel they are not being listened to. They will feel alienated, lose ownership, and then bail out. That statement has some validity when dealing with the chronically dissatisfied that we can never please. However, there's adequate room for many types of people to join in a variety of worship expressions in one church. We are choosing to see what God can do across the generations.

Our commitment is still for a relevant and **sensory** experience in worship but with an **eclectic** design. We use different instruments (guitar, drums, bass, piano and synthesizer, flute, congas, saxophone, violin, mandolin, tambourine, and harmonica), different art forms (drama, dance, banners, streamers, prophetic singing, Scripture reading, creeds, communion) and different musical sources (Vineyard, Hosanna, Martin Smith and Delirious?, Kevin Prosch, traditional hymns, and songs written by worship leaders that have come from New Life: David Ruis, Andrew Smith, Norm Strauss, and Malcolm Petch). We have even adapted some secular songs to a worship or devotional context. For example, while we listen and 'identify' with the lyrics, our worship teams have sung songs like the Eagles' *Desperado* and James Taylor's *Fire and Rain*. We have sung (believe it or not) Elvis Presley's *I Can't Help Falling In Love With You*. These were very meaningful times of worship and devotion.

We cannot pit 'traditional' against 'contemporary' because both are culturally valid. If our children do not grow up in the church experiencing time-honored traditions such as hymns, creeds, prayers, instrumentation and art forms along with contemporary songs, we will deprive them of key dimensions of our great Christian worship heritage. We should be adaptable. The congregation must be able to easily sing the songs. If they are too complex, hard to remember, or theologically off, people will withdraw and listen rather than participate. Jack Hayford warns upcoming worship leaders to write and sing **simple** songs for the heart.

My wife and I had a great breakthrough in worship during a 'Knowing God' conference sponsored by the Navigators in Colorado. The keynote speaker was Eugene Peterson. He was excellent. However, to be honest, my spirit was more deeply touched by the worship ministry of John Elliot before Eugene's teaching. John Elliot is a worship leader and song-writer based in Nashville, Tennessee. He led us with very simple and traditional songs with only a piano. God's presence was so strong during those times that I spent the better part of the worship on the verge of tears, silence and awe. John was as effective in releasing the Spirit than almost any 'renewal' worship experience I've had. He led worship in spirit and truth with celebration and devotion.

Wrestle with Celebration and Devotion

Certain personalities, worship leaders and churches lend themselves usually to one end of the spectrum or the other – strong on celebration or strong on devotion. The younger set usually desires more upbeat celebrative worship. The older set usually desires more devotional worship. Don't we need a balance of both regardless of generation? Celebration grants festive joy and excitement. Devotion provides time for reflection, adoration, and quietness. Too much celebration and people wear out. Too much devotion and people get bored. Too much spontaneity and people become disoriented. Too much structure and people become frustrated. To stoke the flames of a revived church also requires great worship with the help of priests, pastors and prophets.

Wrestle with Priests, Pastors and Prophets

I'll never forget the Wednesday evening meeting where we invited our whole worship community to discuss the vision and values of the worship area. We had gone through another season of 'wrestling with worship.' My view is that the worship leader and teams are first **priests**, then **pastors**, then **prophets** (in that order). As 'Levites' in temple worship, they are called to **serve** the church in worship as they **mediate** God's presence (priest), **shepherd** the church (pastor), and act as a **voice** to the church (prophet). It is primarily about **servant leadership** not about musical anointing or gifting.

However, I have seen worship leaders either reverse the order or not give due attention to a couple of the elements. At that meeting, one of our leaders got up and said that he believed the worship community's role was to be a 'prophetic disruption.' Yes, the worship community's role has a prophetic dimension to it, as it seeks to channel God's voice to bring awareness to our culture and our complacency. Artists, poets, musicians, actors, and the creative arts often provide social and spiritual commentary on the times. But in the Christian realm they will be heard more if they will express it through servanthood, submission, and team-work. They must also be willing to work with pastors and people where there is mutual esteem, safe relationship, and humility empowered through unity of vision and values. Otherwise, what we will get is prophetic **destruction**.

Ultimately, God's heart is to see worshippers who do not come to the temple empty-handed (Deuteronomy 16:16–17). The crucial motive in worship is to give rather than to get, to serve rather than to be served. As we place ourselves on the altar as living sacrifices holy and acceptable to God (Romans 12:1–2) and continually offer to God a sacrifice of praise – the fruit of lips that confess His name (Hebrews 13:15) – we will with pure hearts, open communication, cultural relevance, celebration and devotion, be empowered to worship in spirit and truth. May I encourage you, as Jacob did, to *'struggle with God and men and overcome'* (Genesis 32:28) and to receive the blessing of God as you 'wrestle with worship' as a revived church.[92]

Chapter 10

Praying with Fire

*'After preaching to an earnest congregation at Coleford,
I met the Society. They contained themselves pretty well during
the exhortation, but when I began to pray the flame broke out:
many cried aloud; many sunk to the ground; many trembled
exceedingly; but all seemed to be quite athirst for God, and
penetrated by the presence of His power.'*[93]
(John Wesley)

When I was an instructor at a Bible College we had weekly staff meetings immediately after lunch. At every meeting we would discuss college business and conclude with about fifteen minutes of prayer. Before we prayed, the academic dean would ask one of us to close the prayer at a natural spot. On one occasion he asked me to close, but I fell asleep during the prayer only to wake up to an awareness that the room was dead silent. I then realized that the whole staff was patiently waiting for me to close! I acted as if nothing had happened and pretended that I was giving plenty of last-minute time for everyone to pray before I concluded. I gave a short closing prayer and the staff heartily said 'Amen!' We went our ways to resume college responsibilities.

How many times have you fallen asleep during prayer or couldn't wait for someone to give the last 'Amen' that mercifully indicated that the prayer was over? Or how many times have you endured the mid-week prayer meeting where everyone submitted their shopping lists, prayed without passion or purpose, went home, and saw very occasional answers? Are our churches sleepy with prayer?

I've seen that largely the Western Church, and also driven people, are not dedicated to the life of prayer (me included). We are busy, self-reliant, and tired. Prayer seems boring and ineffective. We enjoy discussing problems and decisions more than praying about them. Lou Engle of Harvest Rock Church in Pasadena declares that 'We talk to much and pray too little.' But, Jesus flatly declared,

> *'It is written, "My house will be called a house of prayer."'*
> (Matthew 21:13)

Fortunately, prayer is sweeping the nations like a Texas tornado. You'll find Friday all-night prayer watches, prayer marches, prayer summits, concerts of prayer, 40 days of fasting and prayer, prayer evangelism, prayer shields, prayer walks, intercessory prayer, warfare prayer, and revival prayer. Missiologist David Barret estimates that 170 million Christians are committed to pray every day for revival and evangelization, with 20 million claiming that this is their primary calling in the body of Christ. Ten million prayer groups make revival prayer one of their primary agendas, while hundreds of prayer networks are committed to mobilizing such prayer within denominations, within cities, and within whole nations.[94] I would agree with David Bryant who declares that, 'We are standing in the vortex of what may be the most significant prayer movement in the history of the church.'[95] I've discovered an astonishing verse, Luke 3:21. When all the people were being baptized, Jesus was baptized too. **And as he was praying, heaven was opened!** Wow! Prayer can open the heavens! The next verse says the Holy Spirit descended upon Him. Churches must become heaven-opening Holy Spirit power houses of prayer. Just imagine!

Becoming a Power House of Prayer

Imagine your church as a power house of prayer – a place where prayer dwells and lives, not just a place where prayer ministry occurs. Glen Martin and Dian Ginter wrote *Power House: A Step-by-Step Guide to Building a Church That Prays*. They say,

'The true powerful house of prayer will have prayer saturating every aspect of its individual and corporate life. Having significant prayer will be seen as the first thing to do when planning, when meeting, etc. ... People will think of prayer as a major factor to be used at first to solve any problem. The whole congregation will be involved in prayer to some degree. Prayer will have a foundational positioning in the life of the individual and the church as a whole.'[96]

Korean Christians value the power of prayer. Early morning prayer and all-night prayer meetings in the Korean church are normal church life. Thousands are up at 4.00 am, 5.00 am or 6.00 am prayer meetings daily, while thousands more are also at Friday night meetings from 10.00 pm until dawn the next day. C. Peter Wagner reports that,

'Over the past 100 years, Protestant Christianity has grown from zero to more than 30 percent of the population of South Korea ... Of the 20 churches in the world that count weekend attendance of 20,000 or more, 9 of them are in Korea alone. The largest Baptist church, the largest Methodist church, the largest Presbyterian church, the largest Holiness church, and the largest Pentecostal church in the world are all in Korea. David Yonggi Cho's Yoido Full Gospel Church is the world's largest, having a membership of 700,000. How did this spectacular growth happen? Many have asked this question of Korean Christian leaders, and virtually all have received the same one-word answer: **prayer**![97]

George Barna, market researcher of trends in church and society, wrote *User Friendly Churches*. He presents common features of vibrant churches that stood out from others with their ability to positively affect their communities. One feature is prayer. He writes, 'The perceived value of prayer within a church is evident through the ways in which prayer is integrated into the corporate activities of the church.'[98] He concludes, 'In short, prayer was every bit as high-profile a ministry in these bodies as was preaching, counseling, youth ministry and missions.'[99] Thom Rainer of Southern Baptist

Theological Seminary in Louisville, Kentucky studied 576 of the most evangelistic churches he could find in America. He found that 'Nearly 70 percent of the churches rated prayer as a **major** factor in their evangelistic success.' [100]

Praying with Passion

From my library, I've read over 25 books on prayer. But, I don't think they have injected more passion into my prayer life. They have given me helpful principles and increased my vision for prayer and intercession. But the reality is, I must cultivate passionate prayer as a regular experience of my walk and talk with God. Feel the passionate tones of Paul's exhortation:

> 'Never be lacking in zeal, but keep your spiritual fervor, serving the Lord. Be joyful in hope, patient in affliction, faithful in prayer.' (Romans 12:11–12)

Or capture the mood of the church that prayed for Peter,

> 'So Peter was kept in prison, but the church was earnestly praying to God for him.' (Acts 12:5)

The word 'earnestly' means **to stretch out** (with tension) as an athlete stretches for the finish line. Again Paul exhorts, *'Devote yourselves to prayer, being watchful and thankful.'* The term 'devote' means to 'be earnest toward, to persevere, be constantly diligent, to adhere closely to.' This is heart devotion. Praying without passion is like flying without taking off – it doesn't work! Paul Bunyan said, 'When you pray, rather let your heart be without words than your words be without heart.'

Revived churches are praying churches. They pray with passion. In his book *Churches That Pray*,[101] C. Peter Wagner wrote a chapter entitled 'Rhetoric Prayer Versus Action Prayer.' He describes a common ailment in our churches: we **talk** about prayer, **teach** about prayer, and **believe** that prayer is important. But we really don't have a high value on prayer. And we really don't expect answers – in other words, we have abundant rhetoric. Ever been there, done that? Wagner believes that action prayer can:

- Help growing churches increase their growth rate and deepen the spiritual quality of their churches.
- Turn around non-growing churches.
- Change the spiritual atmosphere over the community as a whole for more social justice and evangelistic openness.[102]

To pray with passion also means to pray with purity. Jesus cleansed the Temple so it would become a suitable house of prayer. Without purity, passion becomes mere religious excitement. Purity is the match that will ignite the wood for praying with fire. Humility, fasting, confession, and repentance are ways to foster purity in prayer. For example,

> *'If my people, who are called by my name, will humble themselves and pray and seek my face and turn from their wicked ways, then will I hear from heaven and will forgive their sin and will heal their land.'*   (2 Chronicles 7:14)

> *'If I had cherished sin in my heart, the Lord would not have listened; but God has surely listened and heard my voice in prayer. Praise be to God, who has not rejected my prayer or withheld his love from me!'*   (Psalm 66:18–20)

Purified passion fuels action prayer – where leaders radiate God's fire in them as they stir others to prayer. Eifion Evans quoted this report of the 1904 Welsh Revival, 'Evan Roberts was like a particle of radium in our midst. Its fire was consuming and felt abroad as something which took away sleep, cleared the channels of tears, and sped the golden wheels of prayer throughout the area.'[103] Passionate prayer isn't necessarily prayer with volume and intensity. It's prayer with heart and concern. We'll pray about things that concern us. We have passion for things that matter most. Purpose focuses passion.

Praying with Purpose

Purpose is 'that which one sets before himself as an object to be attained; the end or aim to be kept in view in any plan, measure, exertion, or operation; design, intention.' Praying without purpose is like playing without fun – it doesn't work! Focus on the big picture, dream big dreams, overcome big obstacles, and look to a big God to provide. Without purpose, prayers perish. If your eight-year-old child had terminal cancer you would pray with passion and purpose! For one year, that's what our church did as we asked God to heal our worship pastor's son. To date, his blood is clean and the cancer vanished. During the fall of 1993 our church prayed that the City Council would end their opposition to our desire to purchase our present church facility that was zoned for commercial use. Within one week, instead of taking our case to a judge, they reversed themselves and let us in without a legal battle. These are only two of many cases where we fasted and prayed with fire and God answered!

Our youth pastor, Nathan Rieger, studied in Wales at Rees Howells Bible College for two years to learn about prayer. He had to ask God for something impossible and then to track the answers to that prayer over time. He felt the Lord ask him, without telling anyone, to give away all his money that he had saved up for his two years of school tuition and living expenses. He gave about $6,000 to several needy families in Russia. For two years he trusted the Lord as he literally prayed his finances into existence. There were times where what he needed arrived at the last minute down to the last penny. Wow! It happened. His prayers had purpose and passion.

Define the purpose of your prayers. Are they for cleansing and repentance? Are they intercession for revival? Are they warfare prayers for evangelism and social impact? Are they for healing or reconciliation? Are they for personal needs? Know the purpose then pray with fortitude.

Pray with Fortitude

> *'Jesus told his disciples a parable to show them that they should always pray and not give up.'* (Luke 18:1)

The spirit is willing but the flesh is weak. We have all said 'I am going to get up early so I can pray more.' We try for a few days and then go back to sleeping in. Perhaps we need to develop a better theology of perseverance and patience in prayer as we really get in touch with our felt-needs. I guess James felt similarly,

> *'Be patient, then, brothers, until the Lord's coming. See how the farmer waits for the land to yield its valuable crop and how patient he is for the autumn and spring rains. You too, be patient and stand firm, because the Lord's coming is near.'*   (James 5:7–8)

> *'The prayer of a righteous man is powerful and effective. Elijah was a man just like us. He prayed earnestly that it would not rain, and it did not rain on the land for three and a half years. Again he prayed, and the heavens gave rain, and the earth produced its crops.'*   (James 5:16–18)

I determined early on that I would commit myself to regular prevailing prayer. Today, as I write, I am on day 20 of a 40 day fast of water and juice. Man, I feel fortitude as I pray and write. I even have one of Wesley Campbell's CDs on praying the Bible piping through my computer speakers. I'm getting fortified. As Bill Hybels, pastor of a 16,000 member church writes, '**I'm too busy not to pray.**' I usually get up an hour early each morning for prayer and Bible reading and pray throughout the day as I drive and walk. For the past two weeks, my wife's mother has been in hospital recovering from severe flu and pneumonia. She was on the edge of death a couple of times. Talk about praying with fortitude and fire! We prevailed for her and now she is out. C. Peter Wagner remarks that Chinese Christians have a widespread motto: 'Little prayer, little power, no prayer, no power.' [104]

Pray with Focus

How can we pray and not give up? Focus. General prayer gets general answers. Focused prayer gets specific answers. Arthur Wallis remarks that, 'Much ineffectiveness in prayer is caused by the vagueness of the request. If water is allowed to flow at random over a wide area it will dissipate its energy and produce only a marsh. If confined to a river-bed its power may be harnessed to turn a mill or generate electric power ... There is a place and time in military strategy for general harassing tactics, but when the moment arrives for attack and advance, success depends on the concentration of force at the strategic points.' [105]

By the time he reached age 25, Evan Roberts had prayed for thirteen years for a move of God's Spirit in Wales. In 1904, he had a vision and asked God for 100,000 souls. God answered that prayer with the Welsh Revival that brought in 100,000 souls. It also affected other places such as the UK, India, Europe, Asia and North America. John Kilpatrick of Brownsville Assembly of God in Pensacola, Florida also prays with focus. For $2\frac{1}{2}$ years, he and his church met for weekly Sunday night prayer only services to pray for revival. God answered on Father's Day, June 18, 1995, when Stephen Hill gave his first message with an altar call. Before he preaches at the revival meetings, Stephen Hill summons 2,500 people crammed in the church building to pray the following prayer, 'Dear Jesus, speak to my heart, change my life, in your precious name, amen.' By late April 1998, over two and a quarter million visitors have attended the revival services with about 133,000 coming forward for salvation. Focused prayer changes lives.

Two of our women intercession leaders, Donna Bromley and Louise Roberts-Taylor both received identical revelation from the Lord about raising up a group of intercessors according to Nehemiah's twelve gates in Jerusalem. They felt directed to recruit a captain for each gate who would then recruit others to comprise a team of intercessors to pray for specific areas. The following are the teams of over 150 intercessors who comprise *The Gatekeepers*:

1.	*The East Gate*	Worship and Arts
2.	*The Horse Gate*	Missions
3.	*The Sheep Gate*	'3–30s' – Children, Youth and Young Adults
4.	*The Healing Gate*	Support Groups, Counseling and Healing
5.	*The Old Gate*	Conferences and Schools
6.	*The Fountain Gate*	Care Groups

7.	*The Water Gate*	Pastor's Prayer Shield
8.	*The Prison Gate*	Emergency Prayer Chain
9.	*The Fish Gate*	Evangelism and Revival
10.	*The Ephraim Gate*	Men's and Women's Ministries
11.	*The Inspection Gate*	Administration and Finance
12.	*The Valley Gate*	Church Body at large

Through *The Gatekeepers* we are trying to bathe our church and community in intercession. We also believe in church unity as a form of intercession. As we move away from denominationalism to post-denominationalism – where church loyalties are more to our communities and to other churches than to our denominations – we will see more fullness in prayer. When we gather to pray with other leaders and churches we will see the effects in our churches and communities. Local pastors carry the ultimate spiritual authority in a city as 'spiritual gatekeepers.' The power of unity with these people is profound. This unity can come when local pastors worship, confess, and pray together. As they break dividing walls of theology, denominationalism, and isolationism, God commands a blessing through unity (Psalm 133).

Every year we have at least two, day-long prayer retreats where pastors from various churches gather to share hearts, confess sin, and pray for each other's churches and our community. Several churches also have various weekly prayer meetings that are interdenominational in attendance. Currently we are working to build a 24-Hour House of Prayer where leaders from many churches head up a team of intercessors who agree to pray in one hour slots around the clock. These are only a small sampling of what's occurring around the world with pastors praying together.

Praying Our Cities and Nations to God

Perhaps the 90s will go down in church history as the decade of prayer. Hundreds of books seminars and conferences on prayer and intercession are saturating the world. John Dawson of Youth With A Mission (YWAM) came out with his book *Taking Our Cities For God* in 1989. In it he presents five biblical principles that give helpful focus and purpose to warfare prayer for our cities:

1. Worship,
2. Waiting on the Lord for insight,
3. Identifying with the sins of the city,
4. Overcoming evil with good, and
5. Travailing until birth.[106]

His book shows how churches can participate in strategic intercession for their communities. Others like Ed Silvoso, C. Peter Wagner, Cindy Jacobs and Argentinean evangelists Omar Cabrera and Carlos Annacondia go further in warfare prayer. They engage in 'spiritual mapping', naming principalities and tearing down spiritual strongholds in a city. This is experimental and controversial, yet it shows we have come a long way from mid-week prayer meetings to a lifestyle of revival 'praying with fire.' People like Mike and Cindy Jacobs pray for nations like most of us pray for people. Warfare prayer and revival prayer can move a nation.

I sat stunned, as I watched a video of the 1991 inauguration of Zambian President Frederic Chiluba and a later address he gave to a crowd gathered to mourn the death of the entire Zambian soccer team whose plane had crashed. By an open declaration he dedicated Zambia to the Lord and His Word as a Christian nation. He interceded for Zambia with passion and purpose. That declaration became incorporated into the Constitution. That was historic!

Several months later, I sat in my office with Pastor Derek Mutungo of River of Life Ministries in Ndola, Zambia. With his piercing eyes, he recounted his vision for church growth and renewal, city and nation-wide intercession, and equipping the laity to enact the values of Christ's kingdom in Zambia. He has pledged himself to help fulfill President Chiluba's vision of building a nation on the Lordship of Jesus Christ and the Bible. He believes that Africa can reap massive personal and social fruits by yielding itself as a nation to Christ.

We talked of the election of Mr Chiluba. I asked, 'What part did intercession have in that election?' Derek replied, 'The president was virtually prayed into office.' Derek told me how thousands of Zambian Christians fasted and prayed and participated in all-night prayer watches for their nation and the election. God heard their prayers. Many social, political, economic, and spiritual improvements are happening in Zambia today. The Zambian Christians believe you can pray your nation to God. What about you and me? What about America? What about your nation? As Walter Wink states, 'History belongs to the intercessors.' [107]

At one of our Thursday morning intercession times, Donna Bromley, while waiting on the Lord, saw mist rising to heaven and coming back down again to earth as rain. She was directed to the following passage,

> *'How great is God – beyond our understanding! The number of his years is past finding out. He draws up the drops of water, which distill as rain to the streams; the clouds pour down their moisture and abundant showers fall on mankind. Who can understand how he spreads out the clouds, how he thunders from his pavilion? See how he scatters his lightning about him, bathing the depths of the sea. This is the way he governs the nations and provides food in abundance. He fills his hands with lightning and commands it to strike its mark.'*   (Job 36:26–32)

She felt the Lord was saying that intercession is like mist that rises to Him in heaven, which He gathers up and sends back down upon people as rain. She also felt that intercession is like lightning which the Lord gathers in His hands and hurls down to strike its mark. The actual Hebrew word for 'strike' is *paga*. It is also translated as 'intercession'. Prayers that rise as incense before the Lord in heaven and return as fire from the altar, striking the earth with thunder, lightning and an earthquake are seen in the apocalyptic imagery in Revelation 8,

> *'Another angel, who had a golden censer, came and stood at the altar. He was given much incense to offer, with the prayers of all the saints, on the golden altar before the throne. The smoke of the incense, together with the prayers of the saints, went up before God from the angel's hand. Then the angel took the censer, filled it with fire from the altar,*

and hurled it on the earth; and there came peals of thunder,
rumblings, flashes of lightning and an earthquake.'

(Revelation 8:3–5)

To stoke the fireplaces of a revived church means we will pray with fire. Maybe you will be the next Evan Roberts or John Kilpatrick. We must each become walking, talking, power houses of prayer. Then God will strike the mark and the earth will shake with His glory.

Chapter 11

When We Come Together...

'What then shall we say, brothers? **When you come together***, everyone has a hymn, or a word of instruction, a revelation, a tongue or an interpretation. All of these must be done for the strengthening of the church.'*
(The Apostle Paul, 1 Corinthians 14:26)

While driving home from a Sunday morning service, I reflected on what we as a church had just experienced together – God's presence. It began with the opening prayer and continued through the worship, the message, and the prayer ministry at the end. It was like that feeling you get when all you can say is, 'Wooooooooo!' As we concluded the worship I felt impressed to lead the church in silence and simply wait on the Lord. As we waited, a 'holy hush' settled upon us – even among the hundreds of small children. Then one of our worship team vocalists burst forth in a prophetic song. The hair on my arms stood up as I got goose bumps. The Presence intensified.

We continued to wait. I prayed silently and wondered, 'What next?' The only answer I **felt** was 'Continue to worship.' I then quietly asked our worship leader if he would lead us. We worshipped, gloriously! As we did, I faced the reality that **our** plans for the service had been altered. I thought, 'What do we do now?' The only answer I **felt** was 'Preach.' I checked with the other pastors to tell them what I felt and we consulted on how we would lead the revised service – or should I say, how we would let **God** lead it.

As I prepared to preach, I **felt** led to pray. After that, I asked the parents to dismiss their children quietly to Sunday School while I began to preach. I had been preaching a series through 1 Samuel. As a church we were learning about **and experiencing** brokenness, submission and obedience. As part of my message, I invited a young woman to share the story of what she had learned while at a Youth With a Mission DTS (Discipleship Training School) and outreach in Guyana. She told of brokenness, submission and obedience!

As I preached on Jonathan and David from 1 Samuel 20, I developed the theme of covenant friendships and relationships. With unction and authority, the Lord made heart connections and relevant application to our people as my mind and heart flooded with ideas and illustrations. At the end of the service, a woman showed me a book she had been reading and had brought to church for some reason that morning. Its title was *Covenant Relationships* – it also dealt with Jonathan and David!

After my message, we celebrated with a final song and invited people to come forward for prayer ministry. There were some emotional and physical manifestations but nothing inappropriate or distracting. Much of the service was a magnificent mingling of gentle weeping with a sense of 'holy awe.' God was there! He knit everything together like a colorful tapestry.

What was the difference between this service and other services? God amazingly led this meeting as we made space for Him to do so. This service might never have happened if we had simply gone with our own agenda, and most people would not have noticed the difference. How important is the difference anyway?

As I drove home, I thought, 'How do you know when God's there?' My answer, 'Sometimes people cry, sometimes they laugh.' Why? Because God touches the heart where there is so much pain as He heals the emotions where joy can flow. How do you know when God's there? You **feel** his presence. You sense a thickness in the air, or a prickly 'buzz.' You feel the weight of His penetrating holiness and love. You experience an atmosphere charged with glory. My purpose is to be a godly leader and be a pillar in a revived church for the 21st century. How about you?

The 21st Century Church

What will people look for in a 21st century church? An **experience** of God's supernatural presence. The successes of the Charismatic and Pentecostal movements along with the New Age movement show that people are interested in the supernatural and spiritual. Oxford researcher David Barret estimates that by the year 2000, 26 percent (554 million) of the world's 2.1 billion Christians will be Charismatic and that by 2025, 37 percent (1.1 billion) will be Charismatic [108] – unless, of course a global revival hits before then. Conservative evangelical denominations are plateauing and mainline denominations are declining in numbers. Why? I believe that evangelicals, infected by rationalism, typically lack genuine encounters with God's supernatural presence. Mainliners, infected by liberalism, lack not only the supernatural but also the authority of sound Bible teaching. Basing church life on doctrine or a social gospel will not cut it. Says Leith Anderson,

> 'People tell me they are looking for a church where they can meet God, where there is the power of the Holy Spirit, and where their lives can be radically changed. We have a generation that is less interested in cerebral arguments, linear thinking, theological systems, and more interested in encountering the supernatural.' [109]

Designing Meetings That Connect with God and People

As we come together for church services much depends on prior preparation through defining purpose, engaging in prayer, and effective planning. What is your purpose for Sunday morning? Is it evangelistic and geared primarily to non-Christian seekers? Is it celebrative and geared to Christians? Do people primarily get information, inspiration, instruction, or what? Who is your target audience and what are their needs? We must define the purpose of our churches but also the purposes of our meetings.

At New Life we feel that our primary target is those people in our sphere of influence who are what we are. Our purpose is to experience God's presence in worship, inspiration, instruction, and prayer ministry. So, we have eliminated most announcements, keep the service flowing with a positive atmosphere, structure for spontaneity, and preach and pray with passion. We use contemporary worship and art forms, pray for people, and practice open worship, open sharing and open ministry.

At staff meetings each week, we also pray through the upcoming Sunday services and plan them according to our purpose. We also evaluate the previous Sunday according to our values and vision and reinforce the positive elements as we consider options to improve the negative elements. A team of intercessors regularly prays for the upcoming services and for the worship team and speaker. They often pray during the services. You can tell the difference. As we plan the content and structure, our goal is to have one that's flexible and open enough to allow the Holy Spirit to lead us into unexpected areas on the spot.

Music and Worship

When we come together, what is the purpose of the music and worship? It should not be to just prepare for the preaching. Any word study in the Bible will quickly show that music and worship is central to approaching the Lord and entering His presence. Worship is the place and posture of reverence, sacrifice, and ascribing honor and 'worth' to God. Music and worship are the language and art-forms of the Spirit that help us connect with God in celebration and devotion. Through worship (and praise) we place the Lord as King in our lives. Notice Psalm 22:3,

> *'But You are holy, enthroned in the praises of Israel.'*
>
> (NKJV)

> *'Yet Thou art holy, O Thou who art enthroned upon the praises of Israel.'*   (NASB)

Bob Sorge describes it well, 'He is made King when we praise Him, for we are declaring His Kingship and Lordship to a world that does not recognize Him as Lord. By singing, "He is the King of kings, He is the Lord of lords," we are testifying to the heathen (and to the saints, too) of His Lordship and thus are "enthroning" Him with our praise.'[110]

When we come together, our goal should be *'To sing out the honor of His name; make His praise glorious'* (Psalm 66:2 NKJV). To 'sing out' and to 'make his praise glorious' means that we are to put passion and focus into our worship. Something 'glorious' has great beauty, and splendor. Boring, unemotional, and ritualistic music and worship are not glorious. We must 'make' His praise that way! Perhaps we should ask not 'what did I get out of the service?' but 'what did I give to the service to honor and ascribe worth to God?' A.W. Tozer declared, 'Christians don't tell lies, they sing them in their hymns.'

As we gather, we place music and worship as a central end in themselves. All revivals both biblical and historical experienced a revival of music and worship that released the tangible experience of God's presence. Brian H. Edwards reports,

> 'On Wednesday, 13 August 1727 God came among the small community of exiles at Hernhut on the estate of Count Zinzendorf in Saxony: "A sense of the nearness of Christ was given to us all at the same moment ... what the Lord did for Hernhut, from that time till the winter of the same year, is inexpressible. The whole place appeared like a visible tabernacle of God with men." One report of the revival in Cambuslang in 1742 speaks of a "gracious and sensible presence of God." Over a century later in Wales we meet the same word: "The house was often so full of the divine presence that ungodly men trembled terror-stricken ... During the 1904 revival people could feel the presence of God even at a distance from a town; it was something felt and tangible" ... In January 1907, when God came down among his people in North Korea a missionary records;

"Each felt as he entered the church that the room was full of God's presence ... That night in Pyungyang ... [there was] a sense of God's nearness impossible of description."' [111]

I'd have to agree that 'this 'presence of God' defies human explanation, but it accounts for the exceptional experiences of revival. It is also this ingredient today that is so sadly absent from our meetings.' [112]

The Creative Arts

Part of the revival of music and worship is a **renaissance** of the creative arts for God's purposes through Christians and churches. There have been many famous composers, musicians, dancers, writers, poets, actors, sculptors, painters and artists who used their talents for God's glory. Names like Handel, Bach, Milton, Dante, Michelangelo, Rembrandt, Giotto, T.S. Eliot, C.S. Lewis, Madeleine L'Engle, Bruce Cockburn, U2, Martin Smith and Delirious?, are likely familiar to you. Johann Sebastian Bach (1685–1750) wrote the letters *SDG* (*Soli Deo Gloria*) 'to God's glory alone' at the bottom of his compositions.

The purpose of music, the performing and visual arts, is to bring glory to God as they bring pleasure to the audience. 'Martin Luther is reported to have said that God gave us five senses with which to worship Him and that it would be sheer ingratitude for us to use less.' [113] Have a look at the sights, sounds, color, motion, and emotion in the worship account depicted in Revelation 4. Talk about the creative arts in heaven!

Perhaps you are a creative artist. Does your church honor and use the creative arts effectively in worship settings? If not, maybe that's a good topic for discussion with the pastor sometime. They can inspire and instruct in God's ways while they also interpret experience.

'But Christian art ... must also be interpretation. The artist sees and senses a reality and then tries to convey that experience to us in a poem, a play, a song, a picture ... The Christian artist must be an interpreter who helps us to see and understand experience. He is not manu-facturing mirrors that merely reflect what we already see; he is giving us windows through which we may see what we have never seen. He is also giving us doors that open out into new experiences.' [114]

The creative arts can be 'prophetic windows of the soul' which route God's voice through sight, sound, motion, color, and feeling. But let us remember, the form is less important than freedom. Form isn't important in itself, but only its ability to serve as a vehicle (the wineskin analogy) for freedom. The arts are critical because they carry the word in symbol. At New Life we've used many creative art forms in our worship services: dance, flags, banners, tambourines, drama, and instruments. At times we've also used incense, lamps, visual aids, and props. We have intercessors that have made banners to hang in the worship center. We also have several people who have formed artist's and writer's guilds in our church. We have sponsored art shows as well as a worship and performing arts school and conference. We also produce dramas during Christmas and Easter. Our vision is to integrate music, the creative arts, and even video and media projection, into the natural context of the worship and ministry of the church.

Perhaps we are far too dependent on words in our culture. We are left-brain dominant and rational. Symbols are important if we are to reach right-brain people and busters and to some extent all of us. Listen to E.B. Browning:

> Earth's crammed with heaven,
> And every common bush alive with God;
> But only He sees who takes off his shoes,
> The rest sit round it and pluck blackberries.

High standards are important for music and the creative arts in worship. Whatever we use should contain or reflect sound biblical and theological content. It should also be technically excellent, appropriate, chaste and balanced. The central purpose must be to give attention to Jesus Christ for ministry rather than to the creative artist for performance. The artist and art form must decrease in order for the Lord to increase.

The 'Open' Church

Our church has some great meetings. For years our wineskin contained the wine. Our basic Sunday service structure was: Worship, Announcements, Break, Share and Care, Sermon, Prayer Ministry. Gradually we began to receive regular groans from people who wanted us to free up the services and let God move. This was almost an insult – as if we never let God move. But week after week we found ourselves feeling that we had a hardened structure that no longer served us. Some key people began to say, 'Can't we leave some room for God?' We had little flexibility. We had little life and Spirit in our Sunday services. They were becoming like a slick 'show' or 'program' – words that are anathema for revived churches!

Then God began to surprise us with spontaneity. For example, during worship, a singer would go off on a glorious prophetic song. Sometimes after worship there would be a holy hush in the room where all we could do was just wait in silence – even children! On different occasions, people would accept Christ as Savior after hearing a message that was not even 'evangelistic' or because they cried all through the service with no explanation.

On one unplanned occasion, our children's pastor had publicly welcomed a man in the congregation who had come for the first time. He was the emergency doctor who tried to save the life of a little boy in our church that tragically died as a result of jumping off my front retaining wall while playing with our boys. Our children's pastor broke into tears as he tried to greet him from the front. At that moment the mother of the little boy came to the stage and then invited the doctor to come forward. They explained how the Lord used that tragedy to bring the doctor to salvation. It all happened spontaneously. We could have never planned it for effect. That Sunday was a strategic step for our church to becoming more open.

As God nudged us towards a greater openness, a friend of mine also directed me to a book by James Rutz called *The Open Church*.[115] Rutz's appeal – drawing from first century models – is for open worship, open sharing and open ministry. In other words, a call to more participation from the people rather than solely from the platform and the pastors. While I don't agree fully with Rutz's negative appraisal of 1900 years of church history, his principles are helpful. The principles work better in smaller churches, house-churches and small groups, but can be adapted for larger churches. The Apostle Paul hints at 'open church' when he says,

> *'What then shall we say, brothers? When you come together, everyone has a hymn, or a word of instruction, a revelation, a tongue or an interpretation. All of these must be done for the strengthening of the church.'*   (1 Corinthians 14:26)

We have adapted a modified approach to the 'open church' idea by allowing for more spontaneity in following the Holy Spirit's lead. We still plan certain things like preaching and some sharing items. We try to allow freedom for the worship to go unhindered, and for people to come to the microphone to pray, give a prophetic word, or lead us in prayer or intercession. Sometimes we have to call 'verbals' on the spot to alter the plans, but at least there is never a dull moment. Not long ago God took over in worship. As we ramped up with intense passion while singing some David Ruis and Martin Smith songs, the place exploded! We basically decided to go for it and worshipped for the entire second service – 90 minutes non-stop without a sermon or dismissing the children for Sunday school! At the end, everyone looked stunned! And I still had to take the morning offering! That went down like a coke with no fizz left.

Now Concerning the Collection for God's People (1 Corinthians 16:1)

All churches face the ominous challenge of how to meet expenses with an unpredictable flow of weekly tithes and offerings. In fact in 1995, US church members gave only 2.46% of their income to their churches. In 1968 the figure was 3.11%.[116] Perhaps too many pastors and church leaders become preoccupied with counting heads and offerings.

There is however, a fine line between budgeting by faith or by foolishness. Where God speaks or leads, we can budget by faith. Where He doesn't, we budget by foolishness. No matter how we raise money, our approach must place the kingdom of God first (Matthew 6:33) – individually and corporately – and must have the blessing of God in it to succeed (Proverbs 3:9–10; Malachi 3:10; 2 Corinthians 9).

Revived churches will have a revival of giving (see 2 Chronicles 31:4–10). As Brian Edwards remarks, 'For God's people in the Old Testament there was a direct relationship between giving the tithe and receiving the blessing of God. Giving our tithe to God is a necessary preparation if we long for revival, but it is also an inevitable result of revival. When God comes in power he always touches the pockets of his people. In revival there are very few who rob God; on the other hand, spiritual slackness makes people selfish.'[117] But we must first break the 'spirit of poverty.'

The 'spirit of poverty' is a fear of giving because of a fear of not getting. To withhold through fear and lack of faith brings poverty. Proverbs 11:24 says,

> 'One man gives freely, yet gains even more; another withholds unduly, but comes to poverty.'

Romans 14:23 says,

> 'Everything that does not come from faith is sin.'

To break the spirit of poverty means that we will give our stuff away with faith and generosity.

One Sunday God led us to literally give away an entire Sunday morning's offering to two other local churches, and a pastor in Estonia – it came to $12,000. A few weeks later, several of us went to deliver the checks to bless these churches. We then selected on the basis of known financial need. I went with a team to one church and Gord Whyte went to the other church during their morning services. I delivered the check at the conclusion of the service together with words of blessing and prayer for the church. We called the leaders along with the pastor and his wife to come up front to present it and to pray for them. Well, you gotta know that the place was very emotional. They wept like babies and were stunned. The check for $3,000 was exactly what they needed to meet that month's budget. That same morning, someone donated $20,000 toward our own building fund! Now how's that for kingdom finances?! Give generously to your church and may your church give generously. Stoke the flames with your finances. God will bless you. Count on it.

Preaching with Fire

It was said of Charles Finney, 19th century revivalist preacher, 'When he opened his mouth he was aiming a gun. When he spoke bombardment began.'[118] Wow! We need that kind of preaching in our churches. Evangelist D.L. Moody proclaimed that 'The best way to revive the church is to build a fire in the pulpit.'[119] We need preachers who will preach with fire! We also need people who will pray for their pastors.

To preach with fire does not necessarily mean to preach 'fiery' sermons with loudness, emotions, and gestures. Rather, it means to preach with passion, purpose, and prayer. It means to preach more from the heart than the head and more from character than content. It's preaching that's saturated with Scripture not just based on Scripture and it's preaching with heat in the heart and light in the mind. Just as John the Baptist was *'A burning and shining light'* (John 5:35), so today's preachers should have no more heat than justified by the light.[120] It's preaching with **unction**.

Unction gives insight, grasp, and projecting power as it permeates revealed truth with the energy of God.[121] To preach with fire is to preach with anointing – where the church hears another 'voice,' where 'The tone and texture catches up the listener into a world created by truth, which becomes for the moment, at least, more real than the world of time and sense. It is an intangible quality – perhaps more tinged with imagination than with logic – which determines mood and reaches the deeps of the whole person . . .'[122]

How could Jonathan Edwards read from a manuscript – carefully prepared with theological argument – and still rivet his hearer's attention with gripping suspense as he delivered his now famous 'Sinners in the Hands of an Angry God?' How can Billy Graham deliver simple messages about Jesus Christ and while the choir sings 'Just As I am' see multiplied thousands of people respond to the altar call? How could Peter on the Day of Pentecost give an extemporaneous summary of the Old Testament leading to the Lordship of Jesus Christ that 'cut to the heart' of his hearers leaving them to beg, *'Brothers, what must we do?'* (Acts 2:37) Answer: the unction or anointing of the Spirit upon preachers with fire! John E. Riley describes unction this way:

> 'It includes having the sermon that seems the right word for the time; a congregation that seems open to and longing for truth; a mind that is totally alert; a voice that seems trumpetlike; words, ideas, concepts, illustrations that seem alive and dynamic; emotions, powerful yet controlled in the preacher, shared like electricity by the people. And in it all, God, the preacher, and the people seem to be interconnected as to be one.' [123]

The Apostle Paul wrote,

> *'When I came to you, brothers, I did not come with eloquence or superior wisdom as I proclaimed to you the testimony about God. For I resolved to know nothing while I was with you except Jesus Christ and him crucified. I came to you in weakness and fear, and with much trembling. My message and my preaching were not with wise and persuasive words, but with a demonstration of the Spirit's power, so that your faith might not rest on men's wisdom.'*
>
> (1 Corinthians 2:1–5)

How do we stoke the fireplace for fiery preaching? **By heart preparation in prayer and an openness to the Spirit's spontaneous unction**. Listen to this report from Charles Finney's autobiography:

> 'For some twelve years in my earliest ministry I wrote not a word; and was commonly obliged to preach without any preparation whatever, except what I got in prayer. Oftentimes I went into the pulpit without

knowing upon what text I should speak, or a word that I should say. I depended on the occasion and the Holy Spirit to suggest the text, and to open up the whole subject to my mind; and certainly in no part of my ministry have I preached with greater success or power ... It was a common experience with me ... that was surprising to myself. It seemed that I could see with intuitive clearness just what I ought to say; and whole platoons of thoughts, words and illustrations came to me as fast as I could deliver them.' [124]

May people and pastors together prepare and pray, as George Whitefield did at age 20. Then we will see preaching with fire. He was one of the greatest revival preachers of all time. In 1735 he recorded this in his diary, 'My mind being now more open and enlarged, I began to read the Holy Scriptures upon my knees, laying aside all other books and praying over, if possible, every line and word. This proved meat indeed and drink indeed to my soul. I daily received fresh life, light and power from above.' [125]

Going with the Flow

To balance structure and spontaneity, Word and Spirit, requires keen sensitivity to 'the flow.' We can organize and lead our meetings like a chairman using a point-by-point agenda for a business meeting. We will accomplish the task and get through all the planned items but may miss those moments of unplanned or unrehearsed surprise. Or we can organize and participate in our meetings like a maestro who conducts a concert orchestra. Listen to these insights from Isaac Stern on the analogy of conductor and orchestra. He comments:

'The conductor is not a powerful person. It appears so, but it is not so. On the surface it seems that the music is produced by the power of the conductor to tell every-one what to do and when to do it. He may have to do that, but it is not what makes the music. (If he does too much directing, the real music will not be heard, but only his own idea of it). A good conductor does not

merely tell everyone what to do; rather he helps everyone to hear what is so. For this he is not primarily
a telling but a listening individual: even while the
orchestra is performing loudly he is listening inwardly
to silent music. He is not so much commanding as he is
obedient.' [126]

We will still get through the concert, but there will be
emphases and highlights woven in along the way. Perhaps
the Lord has put His anointing on a certain song or instrument or vocalist. Dwell there awhile longer rather than
moving on to the next song. Perhaps the Lord invokes
silence and waiting in between the songs. Stay there lest
you miss what you might 'hear' there. Maybe the Lord opens
a small door of opportunity for ministry, testimony, intercession during the preach. Go with that rather than with the
next point on the outline. Perhaps at the end of worship it's
time to take the offering but a holy hush sets in among the
people. Back off for a bit. Wait, or pray or worship some
more and take the offering later.

Much depends on 'going with the flow.' Again, Isaac Stern
says, 'The conductor conducts by being conducted. He first
hears, feels, loses himself in the silent music; then when he
knows what it is he finds a way to help others hear it too. He
knows that music is not made by people playing instruments, but rather by music playing people.'

Everything Stern does or says is to help the student
become conscious of what the music is. His power as a
conductor is the power of music over him. He knows that
everyone has the potential to become conscious of the
music and everything he does is designed to liberate that
potential. When we come together, we must open ourselves
to the Great Conductor who plays his music through us and
with us. A Revived Church is an orchestra with Jesus as the
Conductor

Summary

As we come together for worship services, let's plan, prepare,
and pray for them according to purpose. But let's also enter

the red zone and develop the best music and worship possible. Let's use the language of the heart in the creative arts. Let's make the structure more open to allow for spontaneity and the Spirit as we preach the Word of God with fire. Leaders must let go of the controls and unleash the saints to do the ministry – with all the bursting creativity that's trapped in the untapped hearts and hands of many. Unbelievers will come in and say, 'Surely God is in your midst.' As we stoke the fireplace of coming together, God's flame will provide lots of heat and light for a revived church.

Chapter 12

Tending the Sacred Fires of Holiness and Healing

'A poet was once asked, "If your house was burning and you could save only one thing, what would you save?" The poet answered, "I would save the fire, for without fire we are nothing." '
(Anonymous)

'You must live with people to know their problems, and live with God in order to solve them.'
(P.T. Forsyth)

In February 1997, Gord Whyte, our Pastor of Counseling and Prayer, taught at a YWAM Discipleship Training school in Honolulu. The Holy Spirit 'showed up' in significant ways. Gord challenged the class with holiness and healing through the power of the Spirit. After Gord left, Lon Kuykendall director of that school, contacted him with the following e-mail. He wrote,

> 'We had a good week last week and had some major breakthroughs with some of the students. One of the Canadian girls who wouldn't give up the Satanic music decided to burn her CDs. She threw two of them into the fire and had a hard time sending the last one in as well. While she was holding the last one, the fire leaped about three feet to the CD in her hand and it started

burning. She then dropped it into the big fire and the ground by her feet then caught fire and burned into the sign of a cross. It was a pretty amazing thing. You can still see the cross burned into the ground. Mel and Raylene saw the whole thing. The Lord did a lot of healing last week and many past hurts and sins were dealt with. It was a very emotional week and lots of tears were shed but it was an excellent follow up to your week. Ryan renounced his tattoo and the Lord dealt with lots of issues like that in people's lives.'

The longer I live the more aware I become of the sin and sickness in people's broken lives. It's incredible the amount of unimaginable pain and junk that people have to cope with. The report you just read is about some **Christian** young people who were set free. These were God-worshipping, Bible-believing, church-going students. They came to a training school to grow in their walk with the Lord and bang, 'power encounters' occurred. The Word and the Spirit, attended by miraculous signs and wonders, set these captives free. Non-Christians are in worse shape! This is what we call 'kingdom ministry.' Both Luke and Paul reported on it.

> ' . . . how God anointed Jesus of Nazareth with the Holy Spirit and power, and how he went around doing good and healing all who were under the power of the devil, because God was with him.'   (Luke in Acts 10:38)

> 'My message and my preaching were not with wise and persuasive words, but with a demonstration of the Spirit's power, so that your faith might not rest on men's wisdom, but on God's power.'   (Paul in 1 Corinthians 2:4–5)

The average conservative evangelical church is, by and large, long on the 'tell' but short on the 'show.' We are good at telling ourselves about God's power. We 'believe' in it, read about it, and we preach on it. But like John Wimber always asked, 'When do we get to do the stuff. Healing the sick, casting out devils, raising the dead?' Dr Michael Brown of the Brownsville Assembly of God wrote a book entitled, *Whatever Happened to the Power Of God: Is the Charismatic*

Church Slain in the Spirit or Down for the Count? [127] I think he's on to something.

I love renewal. I've seen multitudes touched by God for healing, filling, joy, and freedom. But after renewal then what? Where do we go? Here's where we must go – deeper and farther into the open sea of the Spirit. Did you see the movie *Titanic*? Remember the scene where Rose and Jack were 'flying' on the bow of the great ship in the evening? The wind blew through their hair as they stretched out together toward the open sea while that magnificent ship surged ahead underneath and behind them. What a scene! That's where revived churches must go after renewal – out to the expansive seas of holiness and healing by the dynamic power of God's Word and Spirit. But, in Dr Brown's words, 'God must first show Himself holy.'

Tending the Sacred Fire of Holiness

We won't become revived churches without holiness. It starts with you and me. For *'without holiness no one will see the Lord'* (Hebrews 12:14). Moses and the Israelites sang,

> *'Who among the gods is like you, O Lord? Who is like you – majestic in holiness, awesome in glory, working wonders?'*
> (Exodus 15:11)

Peter said,

> *'But just as he who called you is holy, so be holy in all you do; for it is written: "Be holy, because I am holy."'*
> (1 Peter 1:15–16)

Perhaps God is going to send another 'holiness revival' where along with holy laughter we will have holy lifestyles.

What is Holiness?

Holiness, or to be holy, means to be separate or set apart for God. A holy cup is one set apart for God's use. A holy person is one set apart from sin for God's purposes through salvation. The goal of salvation isn't heaven – though that's an outcome – it's holiness. Notice this passage,

'For the grace of God that brings salvation has appeared to all men. It teaches us to say 'No' to ungodliness and worldly passions, and to live self-controlled, upright and godly lives in this present age, while we wait for the blessed hope – the glorious appearing of our great God and Savior, Jesus Christ, who gave himself for us to redeem us from all wickedness and to purify for himself a people that are his very own, eager to do what is good.' (Titus 2:11–14)

Holiness has to do with the heart. The Puritans suggested that 'The heart of holiness is holiness in the heart.' It's not about keeping rules and performing religious duties. It's an undivided heart inclined toward pleasing and fearing God. It's a heart that echoes David's prayer in Psalm 86:11,

'Teach me your way, O LORD, and I will walk in your truth; give me an undivided heart, that I may fear your name.'

J.I. Packer describes it as,

'The center and focus of one's inner personal life: the source of motivation, the seat of passion, the spring of all thought processes and particularly of conscience ... Holiness begins with the heart. Holiness starts inside a person, with a right purpose that seeks to express itself in a right performance ... A holy person's motivating aim, passion, desire, longing, aspiration, goal, and drive is to please God, both by what one does and by what one avoids doing.' [128]

Scottish revivalist Robert Murray M'Cheyne prayed, 'Lord, make me as holy as a saved sinner can get.' Evidently God answered his prayer. It was reported that he was so holy that people wept at the very sight of him in the pulpit or walking down the church corridors. Would we be afraid to pray his prayer? When we pray 'come Holy Spirit' or when we pray for 'fire' do we know for what we are praying? Often we are praying for impersonal power. But the Holy Spirit is a **holy Person**. He would have us pray for personal purity. And so we should, for there are no revivals and revived churches that lack holiness.

How Do We Tend the Sacred Fire of Holiness?

To keep a nice fire going we regularly throw on new logs. In the same way there are habits of the heart that will help us tend the sacred fire of holiness in our lives. There are many habits but I will suggest only three.

1. Fear the Lord

Like you, I've always struggled with the idea of fearing God. How do we do it? It does mean to have reverence for God, but it's more than that. It also means to develop a sense of dread and woooooo! as you think of His character and majesty. It happens to me especially at funerals where I'm reminded that someday I am going to die. The prospect of entering God's presence with my life the way it is right now gives me a fear perspective.

Meditating on the vastness and beauty of creation also helps. Read Isaiah 40–48 and Psalms 103 and 104. Once I was outside at night looking up into the black star studded universe. I was overcome with a sense of dread and awe. Then I asked God that if He noticed me to please send a falling star across the sky. I gazed up and a minute later one did! Well, I thought, maybe that would've happened anyway. Just in case, I asked him to send another one in the opposite direction. You guessed it. It happened! The fear of God gripped my heart. It motivated me to serve and obey Him. To fear God is a highway to holiness and life.

> 'To fear the LORD is to hate evil.'   (Proverbs 8:13)
>
> 'The fear of the LORD is a fountain of life.' (Proverbs 14:27)
>
> 'Let us purify ourselves from everything that contaminates body and spirit, perfecting holiness out of reverence for God.'
> (2 Corinthians 7:1)

We will hate evil more as we reflect on how it causes so much devastation.

2. Practice Lifestyle Repentance

We start the Christian life with repentance and we continue it the same way. To repent is to change our minds and turn away **from** sin **toward** God by making daily choices that say yes to righteousness and no to unrighteousness. It's not just about keeping the 10 commandments or not drinking and committing immorality (though these are included). There are lots of moral people but not many holy people. Repentance is a way of perceiving and exercising the will toward God.

Repentance helps bring freedom from sin and freedom is based in our design. We are free when we function the way we were made to function. Birds are most free when they fly and fish when they swim. People are meant to be holy. It takes a deliberate choice of the will from the heart and humility.

Andrew Murray said, 'Humility is the bloom and beauty of holiness. The chief mark of counterfeit holiness is its lack of humility. The holiest will be the humblest.' Repentance says, 'Lord, I confess and am sorry for my anger, my pride, my selfishness, my impatience, and my lust. I choose to die to them and live in the opposite direction.' Repentance practices the presence of God and considers Him in our daily decisions – both large and small. God does His part too,

> *'Our fathers disciplined us for a little while as they thought best; but God disciplines us for our good, that we may share in his holiness.'*   (Hebrews 12:10)

Remember, 'Sow an act, reap a habit. Sow a habit, reap a character.' It takes a lifetime to build a character but only a moment to destroy it.

3. Cultivate the Spiritual Disciplines

The way of the heart in silence, solitude, prayer, Bible reading, fasting, and worship will heap some good logs on this sacred fire. However they are only fuel for the fire, not the fire itself. The spiritual disciplines can help with holiness but cannot produce it. The Pharisees proved that! External acts can't change contaminated hearts. It requires internal heart surgery by the Spirit. He can use the surgical tools of the disciplines but **He** does the work. We are very action-oriented people who work way too much and contemplate and rest way too little. We must make regular choices to set aside time and to cultivate a heart that walks in these things. You gotta absorb and apply two great books to help tend your fire, Richard Foster's *Celebration of Discipline* and Henri Nouwen's *The Way of the Heart*.[129]

Tending the Sacred Fire of Healing

There's so much to say about healing that I can't hope to deal with it adequately in this chapter. The subject is so vast and important that many books have been written on it.[130] But, from a systemic perspective, revived churches should be **healing environments** where the Word and the Spirit are effectively released to help people become more whole. In fact holiness is even related to wholeness and healing of the whole person – mind, body, and spirit. In the past few years, I've been increasingly convinced that the church as a Word and Spirit community, as a functioning body, is the strategic place where tending the sacred fire of healing can occur. Clinical counseling has a secondary place, but cultivating a healing environment through community, connecting and *charismata* (gifts of the Spirit), have the primary place. I became convinced of this lately after reading two provocative books: M. Scott Peck's, *The Different Drum*, and Larry Crabb's, *Connecting: A Radical New Vision*.[131]

Cultivating a Healing Environment Through Community

There are individuals with gifts of healing (1 Corinthians 12:9) whom God uses to heal people. But just as the church is called to be prophetic or evangelistic it is also called to be a **healing community**. That is, the Word and the Spirit resident in each Christian takes on a collective power and presence when we all do our part to help each other become more whole in Christ. That's how the gifts of the Spirit work for the common good of the whole body (1 Corinthians 12). In other words, healing is not a one-man show. Loving relationships give a proper environment for healing as we impart the life of Christ in us to strengthen and encourage others. Karl Rahner stated that 'The church is the place where the gathered weakness of man becomes the gathered power of God.' Don't you love that? The present Enlightenment church values individuality and rational work. The emerging Post-modern church values community and relational work.

In our fast-paced society where the information available now doubles every two years, technology, travel and television become soul friends for thousands of lonely, depressed people. Genuine community is rare. People need people. They need relationships and places to belong. Jim Wallis remarks that 'Community is the place where the healing of our own lives becomes the foundation for the healing of the nations.' Recovery and support groups are so effective because they are community based and there is a sense of belonging, self-disclosure, study, confession and prayer. Often, not always, physical ailments are caused by spiritual and emotional ailments. Rather than trying to fix people, or solve their problems, ordinary, psychologically untrained people, have enough of God's power to help change others.

One weekend, I was at one of our men's retreats. Several guys shared some pretty deep stuff. One man, a longstanding member of our church, spoke about his hidden addictions to pornography. With tears, he recounted how for years he had battled against pornography with no relief. He tried to make himself accountable to several people who provided no follow-up or help. He unsuccessfully strived to overcome the burning addiction through religious devotion.

Finally, out of desperation, He challenged God as to whether He was big enough to deliver him. He was prepared to go in front of the church and confess it if that's what it would take for God to deliver him. But God said, 'You don't need to do that, just join a men's recovery group and that will do.' So he did. In that recovery group, the men came around him in love and acceptance. Through the Word and Spirit they eventually discovered and cast a demon of pornography out of him. He's been free ever since. He experienced a healing environment through a men's recovery group based on genuine community.

A liability of clinical counseling is that it is a paid service with a one-on-one relationship between two strangers.

There's the counselor and the counselee, detached from a healing environment of loving community. The early church had each other with the Spirit working through each part of the body to bring life and health to the whole. They had no professionally trained healers or counselors. It's interesting that Rick Warren, Senior Pastor of the 15,000 member Saddleback Valley Community Church in California, decided to **not** have a counseling center. Instead they've trained about fifty lay people to do biblical counseling, along with a standard list of approved therapists they can refer to if need be. I think Bill Hybels of Willow Creek Community Church went the same route with his 16,000 member church.

Cultivating a Healing Environment Through Connecting

Here's where Larry Crabb comes in with his book *Connecting*. After 25 years of working as a trained professional therapist, he has concluded that the majority of emotional and spiritual disorders are not the result of damaged psyches but of **disconnected** people. I believe he's right. The path to healing and holiness is honestly connecting or reconnecting with God and His Body, the Church (the great commandment – worship God and love people). Crabb formerly depended on 'fix what's wrong and do what's right' approaches to promote change in people. But he now believes more in the Spirit dynamic of hurting people connecting with God's life that He pours out through His church in **healing relationships**. A lack of togetherness is a root of many people's problems.

Crabb's thesis is 'When two people **connect**, when their beings intersect, something is poured out of one and into the other that has the power to heal the soul of its deepest wounds and restore it to health.'[132] We have the power of Christ within us to connect with others. This kind of relating depends on the church to enter into a deep fellowship with Christ that spills over to other people with the power to change their lives. This is soul care and true discipling. It's not enough to get people to believe or do what's right. We may promote good behavior but still not nurture good health and maturity. Scolding sinners or fixing psyches won't heal them. Being 'present' and focused with people empowers them.

The root of many problems is disconnection not disorder. How do you help a rebellious teen, an anorexic girl, a workaholic father, a depressed housewife, a single adult obsessed with pornography, or an alienated married couple? More often than not, these people are empty souls starving for life and love. To refer them to a counselor might be the wrong prescription. The power found in connection is when life passes between two people. In connecting with God we gain life. In connecting with others, we nourish that life through relationship. Just as the Godhead is a perfect connection between the life of the three members of the Trinity, so connection occurs when the life of Christ in me touches the life of Christ in you. I would not suggest that we do away with counseling ministries, prayer and deliverance ministries, or the use of medication, but we should not rely on these in isolation from community

Communities heal when they see and release what is good in people. Beneath all that bad is the hidden and buried good that must be mined out. Communities heal when they put connecting as the center of life rather than giving good moral advice, insight into problems, or plain encouragement as the center. Sure, people must still resist the bad and release the good – what the Puritans called mortify the flesh and vivify the spirit. God has placed in the body of Christ a tremendous reservoir of healing power.

I received a nine-page e-mail from a friend and fellow pastor who has wrestled with an obsessive compulsive disorder for nine years. He was terrified of contracting the AIDS virus. He got clinical counseling, took medication, received prayer, and tried everything to kick his obsession. He couldn't. Until he realized that he had looked for healing in isolation. He's now living in greater freedom. He wrote,

> 'God has been showing me that changes that truly heal will only occur in the context of biblical community. Attempting to provide healing apart from community is

like trying to fix a broken arm that is permanently disconnected from the body. Before we can effectively extend healing to our lost communities it needs to be an ongoing reality in our church families, for if it isn't we have nothing to extend.'

Cultivating a Healing Environment Through *Charismata*

God also heals in a healing environment through *charismata* – gifts of healing, prayers for the sick and worship (see 1 Corinthians 12; James 5). Many churches have prayer teams and elders who pray for people in their worship services and throughout the week. So do we. We also encourage people to exercise gifts of healing and pray for people in their mid-week care-groups. The more people pray the more results they'll see. We also have a trained ministry team who offer intensive time with people using our 'Set Free' manual. It is similar to Neil Anderson's approach of 'Freedom in Christ' but it goes further. It extends the areas for people to confess and renounce sins and it incorporates a stronger emphasis on deliverance, the gifts of the Spirit, and power encounters. We've helped hundreds of people get healed from many physical, emotional and spiritual infirmities. We also encourage our people in recovery groups to make a 'Set Free' appointment with a team member as part of their healing program.

Lately, we've seen some healing in the context of worship. Our intercession leader Louise Roberts Taylor had lupus for several years. She works at a public swimming pool as an instructor and suffered from constant pain and stiffness in her muscles. Through connecting with many people who gave her lots of love, care and prayer, God finally healed her in worship during a Sunday morning service about eight months ago. She is absolutely radiant and can hardly believe it. On another worship occasion, when our saxophonist played, a grandmother of 23 was healed. For years she could not place her right arm behind her head. As Rikk played his horn, she felt a fire in her chest and later realized she could move her arm all the way around the back of her head. She was healed in the context of music and worship! But some are not healed.

As I write, my heart aches with the reality that one of our long-standing families lost their seven-year-old son to cancer. After a prolonged prayer and medical fight for ten months, he went to heaven. Yes, as a church we prayed – much. Yes, we believe in healing. But no, God did not heal him. Why? Only He knows. It's the kingdom principle of the already and the not yet. He heals some but not all. What will we do now? We will **be there** for the family as a connecting community. We will continue to pray for healing for others when they are sick. We will tend the sacred fires of holiness and healing as we echo the following,

> *'Praise the* LORD, *O my soul, and forget not all his benefits – who forgives all your sins* [holiness] *and heals all your diseases* [healing].'*   (Psalm 103:2–3)

Chapter 13

Spreading the Flame

'Lost people matter to God.'
(Bill Hybels)

'The Church exists by mission as fire exists by burning.'[133]
(Emil Brunner)

Most churches live with an imbalance of trying to fulfill the Great Commandment while neglecting to fulfill the Great Commission. Much of their energy goes toward helping those inside the church to love God and each other better (Great Commandment). Less of their energy goes toward directing that love to those outside the church (Great Commission). This leads to the 'Great Omission.' As Leith Anderson puts it, 'Organizational vision goes in one of two directions – either inward or outward. An organization's first priority is either serving itself or serving others.'[134] With renewal, we will stoke the flames for ourselves, but will we spread the flames to others? We must reach the unchurched – on their turf – more than just invite them on to our turf. We must link ministry to mission outside the church not just to ministry inside the church.

The Church and society are further apart than ever before and many Christians are ill-equipped to bridge the gap. A mission-driven rather than a ministry-driven church will mark tomorrow's churches. These churches will become mission parishes more than pastoral parishes. Harold Percy, Director of Evangelism for Wycliffe College in Toronto, suggests an agenda for mission-driven churches,

The pastoral parish asks, 'How many visits are being made?'
The mission parish asks, 'How many disciples are being made?'
The pastoral parish says, 'We have to be faithful to our past.'
The mission parish says, 'We have to be faithful to our future.'
The pastoral parish thinks about how to save the church.
The mission parish thinks about how to save the world.[135]

How can we build bridges to our community as mission parishes? Below are examples that go beyond the more traditional 20th century 'programs' for evangelism. It begins with **presence**.

Presence Evangelism

The New Testament affirms that the local church and individual Christians are the places of God's presence. The church is the temple of the living God (see Ezekiel 37:26–28; Ephesians 2:22; 1 Corinthians 6:19–20; 2 Corinthians 6:16).[136] Like Moses, we should only want to go where God's presence will be with us.

> 'The LORD replied, "My Presence will go with you, and I will give you rest." Then Moses said to him, "If your Presence does not go with us, do not send us up from here. How will anyone know that you are pleased with me and with your people unless you go with us? What else will distinguish me and your people from all the other people on the face of the earth?"' (Exodus 33:14–16)

God's unique Presence distinguishes His people from all other peoples and religions in the earth. One way tomorrow's churches will reach the unchurched is to be people who radiate God's Presence. Let me illustrate.

One evening a cabinet-maker named Paul was at our home. He came to look at the work needed to finish our kitchen counter tops. Walter, a cabinet-maker in our church, started the job but couldn't finish it. He contacted Hans, another cabinet-maker in our church, to ask if he could finish the job. Hans couldn't finish the job either but suggested Walter contact Paul with whom Hans had worked in a cabinet shop in town. Paul took the job.

We chatted that evening. I learned that he grew up in Southern California as I did in the 1960s. As Paul was leaving, he blurted out, 'Hey you're a pastor in that church on the highway aren't you?' I answered, 'Yes, I'm one of ten pastors.' I could tell he was making a connection point with me. I also knew he was unchurched. We had talked of similar surfing experiences at Southern California beaches. He then asked, 'Do you know Hans? I used to build cabinets with him.' I replied, 'Oh yes, Hans Metzler, I know him. He and Sandy (his wife) are in our church.' Paul remarked, 'Well I used to work with him at a cabinet shop here in town. One day while we were working together I said to Hans, 'You are a Christian aren't you?' Hans had said, 'Yes I am.' After that, Paul said this to me, 'I somehow knew he was a Christian even though he never said anything about it, never preached to me, and never tried to cram religion down my throat even though I probably needed it.'

I then asked, 'How did you know Hans was a Christian?' Paul replied with a smile, 'There was something about a **presence**.' He went on to say that he felt this same presence with Walter and now with my wife and me. Over the next few weeks Paul asked about my Christian life and call to ministry. He was amazed at how he had met two others from the same church whom all carried 'the Presence.' He told me that he was even losing sleep over this and wanted to come to our church 'to listen.' He'd had bad experiences with churches in the past and was turned off. But now he had met three Christians who said nothing yet bore 'a presence.'

Well I eventually invited him to church one Sunday when I gave my complete testimony of darkness to light. After the service I went over to him and sat down. He sat looking very tender. My testimony really touched him. But there was more. He was not having much luck with getting work and planned to move to Tuscon. He really didn't want to. I asked if I could pray for him. He agreed. I could feel the unction of the Spirit as I prayed that God would give him some work the very next week and to allow Paul to stay in our community. When I opened my eyes I saw tears streaming down his cheeks. He remarked, 'You don't know how much that meant to me.' A couple of weeks later I followed up with a phone call. As I prayed with him over the phone I heard a yelp. He said, 'When you pray, I get chicken skin. And I know that's that Holy Spirit.' Yeah, God's empowering Presence! Paul is not far from Jesus. I've invited him to an *Alpha* Course.

Church growth researcher, George Barna, for his book *Evangelism That Works*,[137] surveyed hundreds of unchurched people. He found that most unchurched adults are not enthusiastic about finding a church home but might be if certain appealing conditions were met. The number one factor that would be most appealing is if they could truly **experience God**. People want God. They don't want religion and they don't want church if they can't experience God.

In another example, Dan Unger, a lead guitarist with one of our worship teams and his daughter Juanita, entered a music competition at a local pub. They were ninth on a list of ten acts scheduled for the evening competition. While the first eight did their gigs, the pub was noisy and very few people paid attention. When Dan and Juanita did their three songs, the whole place fell silent. Even the bartender stood captivated. They won the competition and the first prize which was a $2700 Taylor guitar. From our people who went came the report that the difference with their performance was a 'Presence' that gripped people's attention. This is indicative of 'evangelistic worship' that God is blessing with His presence as Christian artists use their craft and become salt and light in their spheres of influence.

Prayer Evangelism

In my opinion, gone are the days of running evangelism primarily through programs and packages. Gone are the days of running mid-week prayer meetings where the saints come with their shopping lists of requests and leave with a feeling that their prayers never got past the ceiling. As never before, Christians are starting to realize that **evangelism is spiritual warfare** where social change, conversions to Christ, and revival will not occur without the weapon of Spirit-led prayer and intercession. C. Peter Wagner warns that 'prayer is not a substitute for aggressive social action or persuasion evangelism. But the best strategies for either will be more effective with high quality prayer than without it.'[138]

Wagner, known for his teachings on church growth, now declares that prayer (particularly warfare prayer) is the first key to church growth, community impact, and reaching our cities for God.[139] Astounding reports are coming in about the effects of praying **for** communities. Concerning evangelism and reaching our cities for God, Ed Silvoso reminds us that without the technological resources available to us today, New Testament believers did a better job than we do.[140] Their key was prayer.

As we pray evangelistically for our neighborhoods we can do likewise for our neighbors. Evangelism is both public and private. Let Paul's appeal in Colossians 4:2–6 form the basis for private prayer evangelism opportunities,

> 'Devote yourselves to prayer, being watchful and thankful. And pray for us, too, that God may open a door for our message, so that we may proclaim the mystery of Christ, for which I am in chains. Pray that I may proclaim it clearly, as I should. Be wise in the way you act toward outsiders; make the most of every opportunity. Let your conversation be always full of grace, seasoned with salt, so that you may know how to answer.'

Donna Bromley, our prayer co-ordinator and wife of Ralph Bromley our missions pastor, felt the Lord lead her to get a membership at a local woman's fitness club called *The Woman's Place*. While exercising there, she then felt drawn to pray for a certain girl on staff named Lori Rockl. For about a year, Donna prayed for Lori and for openings to talk to her about Jesus. At the time, Lori was in a common-law relationship, was an agnostic immersed in New Age culture, and knew very little about Christianity or even the meaning of Christmas.

During this time she attended a week-long encounter group that concluded with a call to commitment to Jesus Christ. For the first time, her eyes opened to the reality of God as she gave herself to the Lord. However, after that experience she continued on with her life with little change.

Later, a friend invited her to our church. It was the same Sunday that our church prayed for Ralph and Donna to go on an outreach to Nepal. Lori sat in the congregation and noticed Donna. When Donna returned from the trip and was back at *The Woman's Place*, Lori asked how her trip went. A surprised Donna asked, 'How did you know we went to Nepal?' Lori replied, 'I was at your church on the Sunday you were sent off.'

This set in motion a relationship where they would have coffee together, go for walks, and play tennis. Donna would teach Lori what her commitment to Christ meant and the lifestyle changes that were necessary for her to walk in God's ways. Ralph and Donna baptized her and Lori eventually moved in to live with them for almost two years. Through lifestyle discipleship Ralph and Donna helped her overcome her past life. She became a member of our church dance team, joined a Bible study with one of the team members, witnessed to her fellow waitresses in the restaurant where she worked and then packed off to South Africa to enroll in a Youth With A Mission Discipleship Training School. Her vision is to become a missionary to Madagascar. A great example of private prayer evangelism that turned an agnostic into a missionary.

'Need Meeting' Evangelism

On the whole, our churches do not attract unchurched people, even though many of them have had church experiences. George Barna discovered that about 85 percent of all unchurched American adults have, at some point, consistently attended a church or religious center. They are not now attending because they were driven away. What was the number one reason they left? Says Barna: 'Those unchurched felt that the church had little real benefit to offer in meeting their tangible needs.'[141] But there is an anomaly. 64 percent say that religion is very or somewhat important to them. Furthermore, 34 percent say they have favorable impressions about Christianity. The story of Jesus and the woman at the well illustrates the point (John 4). As we go about our daily business and travels, we have divine encounters with people with real needs and problems in their lives. In Christ, we are sources of living water who can help meet people's needs.

However, the stumbling block comes down to experiencing that faith in a local church setting. Barna concludes, 'Based on past experiences as well as their current needs and expectations and in spite of their esteem for Christianity, the typical non-churched adult is not predisposed to assume that a local church is capable of delivering on the promises of Christianity and of making the faith come alive. For a church to attract such a person, then, requires bucking the odds.' [142] 21st century churches must build bridges to the community where they can meet the needs of unchurched people who wrestle with life and work. Barna implores, 'Like it or not, the unchurched population is perhaps most open to religion if it can help solve some of their problems or address some of their most pressing needs.' [143]

Some of their most pressing needs are financial problems, employment status, personal health, and family matters. What is startling is that less than 1 percent of them identify any issue of a spiritual nature to be their core concern. [144] Of course many of their problems likely have spiritual reasons. But the church, to be effective, must deal with the social and emotional needs of the unchurched as it seeks to be a voice for the spiritual areas as well. We may need to give a physical cup of cold water before we can talk to the unchurched about their spiritual need for living water. The gospel is social as well as spiritual. We can offer seminars, support groups, and hot-lines to help people. We can also offer our church facilities for need-meeting activities to build bridges between the church and the community.

Seeker-Sensitive Evangelism

Though controversial in nature, an increasingly popular approach for reaching the unchurched is through seeker-sensitive evangelism. Developed by such churches as Willow Creek Community Church in Illinois (Bill Hybels), and Saddleback Community Church in Southern California (Rick Warren), seeker-churches have grown from nothing to over

10,000 in the US since the mid-1970s.[145] The philosophy is to design services that use the performing arts, testimony, contemporary music, and need-meeting messages targeted at lost people rather than at Christians. The goal is for Christians to invite their unchurched friends and family to church.

I believe that both Willow Creek and Saddleback attribute about 80 percent of their growth to conversion rather than transfer growth. In other words, 80 percent of their congregations comprise people converted through seeker-sensitive evangelism rather than through Christians transferring from other churches. The services do require considerable planning and work. We cannot simply be traditional churches and expect non-Christians to want to be a part of it. They don't. Unless we have something very viable to offer, they don't want our religion.

Narrative Evangelism

Post-modern churches face an enormous challenge in how to effectively tell the old gospel story in new ways. Enlightenment Boomer churches focused on the rational defense of the gospel. The goal was to persuade people of the intellectual truth of the Message. But the challenge for tomorrow's church is to model and share the gospel with authenticity and relevance. The Post-modern mindset does not embrace absolute truth. It embraces personal preference. Truth is established through communities and tribal groups who pass on their stories (narratives) from generation to generation (much like the Old Testament). Because stories are an effective method of post-modern communication, revived churches must consider how to use this medium for evangelism.

Jimmy Long states, 'The goal of narrative evangelism is to help the person or people you are talking with adapt their life's story to be more in line with God's story. Thus to become a Christian is to adopt the story of Christ so that we become part of the story-line. Our story becomes a part of Jesus' story.'[146] **It is our personal testimony**. Much like movies, narratives have a personal ring to them. They invite and involve people in the story-line. They play out the truth. The next century generation needs 'to see the incarnation of the gospel in people's lives more than to hear the proclamation of the gospel through our words ... They need to experience the love of Jesus more than they need to be informed that Jesus is love. The key question becomes "Is it real?" not "Is it true?"'[147]

Servant Evangelism

Popularized by Steve Sjogren, Senior Pastor of the Vineyard Christian Fellowship of Cincinnati, Ohio, servant evangelism is an approach to sharing the love of Jesus through 'random acts of kindness' where there's **no guilt**, **no stress**, **low risk and high grace**.[148] He declares that 'Christians and non-Christians have one thing in common: they both hate evangelism.'[149] That's why a 'conspiracy of kindness' can disarm both Christian and non-Christian alike. Steve defines servant evangelism as 'demonstrating the kindness of God by offering to do some act of humble service with no strings attached.'[150] The goal is to not so much **tell** the good news as much as **give** the good news. Methods and programs for evangelism can be confrontational and very impersonal. The church must **be** the good news, **give** the good news, and then **tell** the good news. As St Francis of Assisi encouraged, 'Preach the Gospel all the time, and if necessary use words.'

Spreading the fire should be as much about spreading God's love as God's power. We often compare the Holy Spirit to fire. Clark Pinnock wrote a book about a theology of the Holy Spirit. He entitled it *Flame of Love*.[151] Mother Teresa modeled this 'active flame of love' and said, 'Spread love everywhere you go. First of all in your own house. Give love to your children, to your wife or husband, to a neighbor ... let no one ever come to you without leaving better and happier. Be the living expression of God's kindness – kindness in your face, kindness in your eyes, kindness in your smile, kindness in your warm greeting.'

A number of our people through their small groups and our youth have carried out servant evangelism. They have given away free hot-dogs, cokes, coffee, and even free prayer.

One Sunday, our whole church went out to do servant evangelism as part of the morning service. Each department and small group planned their own activities. Random acts of kindness can come in almost any form: gift wrapping at Christmas, free car washes, popsicle give-aways, snow removal, raking leaves, window and windshield washing, shopping assistance for people who are house-bound, house or yard clean-up, etc. Steve Sjogren gives a full list of ideas in his book *Conspiracy of Kindness*.[152]

One summer, our church had a church picnic at a local park. We cooked and gave away hundreds of hot-dogs and hamburgers to our people but also to a number of other people who happened to be at the park. While we enjoyed our picnic we invited a group of several transients who were there to join us. They loved the free food. Later that summer, one of them, a fellow named Mel Jacoby, decided to attend our church and eventually became a Christian. At our annual men's retreat I talked to him and heard his story. He's now a recovering alcoholic who lives in a discipleship house with several others.

Another fellow, a 27-year-old former drug dealer we call 'Hawkeye,' went from 'lost to leader.' In August 1997, while in a local park, he accepted some free food give-aways from one of our families. Out of politeness to them he came to our church and eventually became a Christian. A few weeks later he met up with Ralph, our missions pastor, who invited him along on a missions trip to Nepal that fall. Well, Hawkeye stayed there for six months and even lived in a remote village for a month teaching and discipling. He returned home for a month, worked, and saved enough money to spend six months helping at an orphanage in Ecuador. The family that originally offered him free food had moved there as missionaries. Hawkeye has his heart set on Asia and perhaps a return to Nepal where he saw many miracles and works of God's power.

Social Impact Evangelism

I have always taught that 'what comes down must go in and out.' In other words, as God revives our churches we must take what comes down from heaven **into** the church and give it **out** to a needy world.[153] We cannot satisfy ourselves with getting 'more.' Argentine evangelist Carlos Annacondia says it well,

> 'I suffer when I see the church so bound up, just receiving blessings for themselves and getting fuller and fuller with the Holy Spirit, going back about their daily lives, then returning to a service a couple days later to get filled again – while the world is going to hell. God told me clearly: the anointing that He is giving to the church is for evangelism. If we don't give that anointing to the lost, it dries up within us. The anointing grows as we give it away.'[154]

A revived church will make a difference beyond its walls. Dr Guy Chevreau remarks that 'As God renews and revives His people in these special seasons of grace, it is as if the wind of His Spirit ripples the pond. The effects of His powerful presence are felt in ever widening circles of influence, often beginning with pastoral leadership, then throughout local congregations, and then beyond the walls of the church.'[155] It will be salt and light (Matthew 5:13–16). Salt is effective only when it makes **contact**. Light is effective only when it is **conspicuous**.

Read virtually any book on revival and you'll get stirred with stories and statistics on how Christians initiated social reform. In revival times, Christians started many of our major missions and benevolent societies. The church made evangelistic impact in society. For example,

> 'Charles Finney believed the Gospel was meant to do more than save people. It was also meant to salvage society. He aligned himself with Arthur Tappan, a wealthy silk merchant, who believed that well-to-do Christians were obligated to give to the kingdom of God. Tappan built teams to form a "Benevolent Empire" of organizations to address the ills of society. By 1834 the annual income of this "Empire" was today's equivalent of 130 million US dollars – which easily matched the major expenditures of the US federal

government. They addressed problems of slavery,
temperance, vice, women's rights, prison reform, and
education.' [156]

We are committed to social impact evangelism. How
about you? Here's one example. In 1994, Ralph Bromley
and John Devries, a businessman in our church, formed a
non-profit society called *Hope for the Nations*. Their focus is
to provide orphanages, hospitality centers or children's
homes for neglected, abused or abandoned children and to
establish profitable business ventures that will lead the
homes in self-funding. The homes and business ventures
employ national workers. The vision is 'To develop today's
orphans into tomorrow's leaders.' With operations in
Liberia, India, Indonesia, Mexico, Nepal, Russia and Bhutan,
Hope for the Nations has about 135 children who will become
adopted into God's family.

Church historian, Richard Lovelace declares, 'It is a clear
lesson of history that there can be no effective social witness
without a revived church.' [157] Christians can stand with the
pro-life movement, serve on school and hospital boards and
in community service organizations. They can influence
Parent Advisory Committees (PTA) or pray for their schools
through *Mothers Who Care*. They can also naturally represent
Jesus in the marketplace.

Dave McLean, a marketing consultant in our church, met
a man for lunch. During the meeting, the man told him of
his marital woes. Dave set aside the business agenda and
asked him if he'd consider asking Jesus for help, prayed for
him, and invited him to church that Wednesday night. He
came. On Friday, with excitement in his voice, the man
phoned Dave to tell him of his decision to accept Jesus as
Savior. He then came to church on Sunday. Dave considers
himself a full-time local missionary. Now that's social
impact evangelism in the marketplace.

Here's another example. Many youth just hang out with
little to do so they get into trouble. God gave Paul Nesbitt, a
building designer in our church, a vision for street youth in
our city. He also loves basketball, so he made a proposal
to our city council to partner with him in building a lighted,

full-size basketball court for youth in our main city park. They agreed and donated $4,000 to the project while Paul raised the rest of the money from churches and private donors. It's part of a city strategy called *Partners in Parks*. His goal: social impact and need meeting evangelism!

Relational Evangelism

No matter how we cut it, relationships form the warp and woof of life. People want to be with people and **community** forms the basis for healthy church experience. Statistics reveal that friends and relatives bring most new converts to Christ. This is called *oikos* (household) 'web,' or 'friendship' evangelism. The Institute of American Church Growth Research in Pasadena, California conducted a survey to determine who or what was responsible for 14,000 lay people coming to Christ. Below are the results:[158]

Through special need	1–2%
Through walk-in	2–3%
Through the pastor	5–6%
Through visitation	1–2%
Through Sunday School	4–5%
Through an evangelistic crusade	1–2%
Through a church program	2–3%
Through a friend or relative	75–90%

Friends and family, work and school chums provide the best context for informal relational evangelism. This produces about 75 to 90 percent of conversion growth in churches. One effective method along these lines is the popular *Alpha* course I mentioned earlier. It's a ten-week practical introduction to the Christian faith designed primarily for non-churchgoers and those who have recently become Christians. Established at Holy Trinity Brompton Church in London twenty years ago, there are now more than 4000 *Alpha* courses in the UK and other countries. Christians can invite their non-Christian or recently converted friends to enjoy a meal, watch a teaching video, and close with an open-ended non-threatening discussion time. We use it and find it very effective.

Cell-groups continue to be a side-door means to reach people. John Wesley used a system of small groups called bands, classes and societies to spread revival and nurture new Methodist converts in England in the 1700s.[159] David Yonggi Cho and the Yoido Full Gospel Church in Seoul, Korea (the largest church in the world with over 700,000 members) uses cell-groups as the primary relational network to reach the unchurched. Each group has the goal to pray for, love and serve two people for Christ per year.

One of our elder couples, Bob and Ruth Young, have led a small group for young couples. Over half of their group were unchurched people they invited. In one example, Bob, an insurance agent, invited his secretary Madeleine to their group. Over time, she became a Christian and then invited her common-law biker boyfriend, Jerry Ashley to the group. Bob also rides a Harley Davidson motorcycle to relate to other bikers. Over time, Jerry became a Christian, then married Madeleine, and made other changes in his biker lifestyle. His friends and clients who would come to his sign making shop began to notice changes in him.

Jerry invited another couple who met in a night-club, James and Barb, to Bob and Ruth's group. James was a tough biker and Barb was a barmaid. Barb eventually came to Christ during one of our Sunday services as I gave my testimony 'From Darkness to Light.' A couple of weeks later, as the entire care-group met together, the Holy Spirit came in mighty power – especially on Barb. As a two-month-old Christian, she accurately prophesied to every member of the group for three hours. The group experienced a profound visitation of God. At 10 minutes before midnight, James gave his life to Jesus. Ever since, he has experienced God's peace and proudly declares that 'God drove the hell right out of me.' This all started as a relationally based evangelistic care-group that ended with power-packed salvations and changed lives.

Revival Power Evangelism

Finally, as we engage in revival power evangelism we will see astonishing results like that described below by Dr Gary S.

Greig. He submitted the following Internet report on Harvest Evangelism's International Institute on Reaching Entire Cities for Christ through Prayer Evangelism Conference, October 31–November 7, 1997 in Argentina.[160]

'Monday 3rd and Tuesday 4th November, 1997

Carlos Annacondia was introduced by Dr Wagner as one of the most powerful evangelists of our time. Annacondia is a nuts-and-bolts factory owner who began to preach the gospel and heal the sick 10 days after he himself came to the Lord in 1982. He has won well over half a million to the Lord since he began. At his crusades people **run** to the altar to accept Jesus, the Spirit moves so powerfully. The anointing of the Holy Spirit is so powerful at Annacondia's crusades that not only do the blind see, the lame walk, the demonized are delivered, but also unsuspecting passers-by have fallen under the power of the Spirit or been healed as they pass the crusade, even though they know nothing of what is going on inside!

When he speaks, the fire of God pierces your soul. He (and God's Spirit) left me and many others weeping as he talked of God's passion for the lost and God's heart for the Body of Christ to rise up in unity and preach the gospel in the streets of the world's cities. He told how just 10 days after he was saved, God called him to preach the gospel and heal those oppressed by the devil (Acts 10:38; John 14:12). Carlos told God he didn't think he could heal or cast out demons because he didn't know how to. But God just told him, "Carlos, don't just believe **in** Me, **believe** Me. Don't just believe **in** My Word, **believe my Word**." *"These signs will accompany those who believe"* (Mark 16:17)...

Carlos then said God told him to go to a hospital in Buenos Aires and preach and heal there. Because it was at the time of the Falkland Islands War, hospitals were under heavy guard by the Argentine military who had posted guards in the hospital to keep unauthorized personnel out. Carlos told the Lord, "If you want me to preach to the sick in the hospital, make me invisible to the guards," and then he courageously walked past two sets of guards who acted as if they did not see him at all!

When he got to a ward with 40 patients, Carlos took his Bible in hand and went to the first bed and asked the person if he could share Jesus with them. The person responded, "I am Roman Catholic" – the patients were nominal Catholics who did not have a personal relationship with the Lord – and turned his head away from him. He got the same response from 39 of the 40 patients until he got to the last bed with a young girl who was paralyzed from the waist down and had been in the hospital many months. Because no one came to visit her for a long time, she began to weep when he came over to her bed, and she welcomed the opportunity to hear about Jesus. After she prayed to receive Christ, Carlos in bold simple faith said to her, "The Lord is going to heal you now," and he raised his hand to lay it on her body and pray for the healing of her paralysis. But before his hand touched her the Lord told Carlos, "She is already healed. Tell her to get up and walk."

Again in bold obedience, he withdrew his hand and told her what the Lord said. She began to weep and tremble under the power of God as she felt God healing her legs. She got out of the bed and began to walk around the bed for the first time in months. The ward nurse saw her and yelled at her, "You're supposed to be in bed! You can't walk!" At the same time all 39 other patients who saw what had just happened all of sudden started shouting at Carlos, "Oh pastor, please come pray for me!" until he was whisked away by the hospital staff.

Carlos Annacondia always *works for unity among the pastors of a city* and prays with the pastors of the city before his crusades, because he feels it is essential for spiritual anointing and authority to preach and heal in the city (see Ephesians 4:2ff; Psalm 133). He has said that when there is a high level of unity among the pastors of a city, that there will be a high level of anointing and power from God on the crusades, and when there is a low level of unity among the pastors of a city, there will be a low level of anointing on the crusade in that city. When he spoke to us, Carlos said that God is worried because millions are dying around the world without hearing the gospel. The Church isn't getting the job done. There are too many diplomas, he said, and not enough preaching the gospel. He added that Satan is scared that the Church will arise **in unity** and begin preaching the gospel in the streets so that revival fire flows in the world's cities. He said that revival begins when a fire starts in the heart of the Church, and a fire starts in the heart of the Church when the Church has the Lord's passion for the lost and the dying. Carlos then said that God is visiting the earth with revival fire.

He said we can't fight the battle with persuasive words alone, we must fight with the power of God's Spirit (1 Corinthians 2:4–5), and we must fight the satanic forces that hold people in blindness – we must order Satan and his forces to **loose** those people they are holding and blinding in the city! Carlos told of how he was sharing the gospel with a family in Argentina and how the mother interrupted him with the remark, "You evangelicals do not honor the Virgin Mary do you?" Carlos replied that evangelicals do honor Mary as the most blessed among women (Luke 1:42), but they do not worship Mary. He went on sharing with the family how Jesus loves them, when the mother interrupted again, "You evangelicals only want money, don't you!" Carlos said he realized the interruptions were a manifestation of a spirit of unbelief influencing the woman, so he asked permission to use their bathroom. In the bathroom, he prayed and rebuked the spirit of unbelief, "In Jesus name, spirit of unbelief, loose this woman and her family and get out of the way! Holy Spirit draw them to Jesus." Then he quietly returned to the family, and he found the mother smiling and beaming at him as she said, "Pastor, please tell us more about Jesus!" She and the others began to shed tears as Carlos shared more about the love of Jesus and as the Holy Spirit moved on them. Finally each of them prayed to receive Jesus personally.

The **purpose of the anointing**, Carlos said, **is to preach the gospel and to break the yoke of oppression**, to release and to heal all those who are oppressed by the devil as Jesus did (Acts 10:38; Isaiah 61:1). He added that signs and wonders and the supernatural work of the Holy Spirit should be sought, expected, and welcomed by the Church when it preaches the gospel to the world.

Dr Pablo Deiros – pastor of the largest Southern Baptist church in Buenos Aires, Central Baptist Church – joined us the first day of the forum. He said that the sustained revival in Argentina is due to an openness among pastors to work and minister together in functional unity with a Great Commission focus. It is also due to pastors recognizing, he said, that the real enemy is not other pastors, churches, or denominations, but that Satan and satanic forces are the real enemy of the Church. The revival is also due, he said, to pastors generally realizing that prayer is the **main** resource for extending God's Kingdom and evangelizing the lost (cf. Acts 6:4; 1 Timothy 2:1–8).

When Dr Deiros was asked why we in North America aren't seeing more revival like Argentina and many other places in the world, he pointed out that besides the general lack of functional unity among pastors in American cities, besides pastors not realizing Satan is the real enemy, and besides pastors not seeing prayer as the main resource for advancing God's Kingdom, the American Church seems to have made the Christian faith, Bible study, etc., too complicated, too religious, and too task-oriented rather than Christ-focused. There is a simplicity of faith in God and His Word that are central to the Argentine revival from the grass roots level to the pastoral level.

Deiros said that until the American Church doesn't just believe **in** God but **believes God** and until it doesn't just believe **in God's Word but believes** His

Word, the American Church will not see widespread revival. He said our vision of God, His Word, and His will is the most important factor that plants the seed of revival in our hearts.

Thursday 6th November, 1997
Claudio Freidzon is a powerfully anointed Argentine pastor who pastors a large Assembly Of God Church In Buenos Aires. He has an anointing like that of Benny Hinn, and God moves powerfully wherever Claudio preaches and ministers. He spoke to international dele-gates at the ministry lunch on Thursday about the four principles which invite the Holy Spirit to come in power and which invite God's Glory into our lives and our churches:
1. Emphasizing holiness, standing against sin and standing for obedience to the Word of God and the Spirit's promptings.
2. Emphasizing the Word of God, grounding ourselves and our congregations in the truth.
3. Emphasizing evangelism: the reason the Holy Spirit moves in power is to evangelize the lost.
4. Emphasizing praise and worship which open the heavens and invite the Spirit to come in power.

Saturday 8th November, 1997
On Saturday about 20 conference delegates went to a Methodist Church In Buenos Aires where Argentine pastors and intercessors were meeting for worship before a public prayer walk around the Plaza De Mayo, the square in Buenos Aires where the main governmen-tal buildings of Argentina are located. Cindy Jacobs, Founder and President of Generals of Intercession and a gifted prophetess, led the prayer walk along with the Argentine leaders. The purpose was for the Argentines to repent corporately for the sins of their nation and the Church which have grieved God, hindered His Spirit, and hindered the Church from fulfilling the Great Commission in Argentina, and to pray that God would send even greater revival to their churches and to the land.

We first prayed that God would bring healing to Argentine families from the loss of family members in the "Dirty War" over 15 years ago when the government of Argentina kidnapped and killed 30,000 citizens in an anti-Communist sweep across the land. We prayed the government would publicly apologize for the atrocities which it has never yet acknowledged publicly. We also joined the Argentine intercessors and pastors in asking God to forgive the sins of corruption, sexual impurity and whoredom, and anti-Semitism in the Church and in the government. Cindy prayed that God would give us **confirming signs** as the Argentine leaders, intercessors, and we delegates prayed through the issues in the Plaza de Mayo.

As we prayed through each of these issues, striking signs occurred – the bell clock on an adjacent building chimed at the beginning of each significant point of prayer, even though the bell was not consistently chiming on half-hours or quarter-hours; the flag on the Pink House (Argentina's presidential palace) went to half-mast and then back up again at another significant prayer point; and there was a literal changing of the guard in front of the Pink House 30 seconds after Cindy Jacobs prayed that God would bring about a changing of the guard in Argentina's government to usher in a government that would stand for righteousness. It was fascinating to see God confirm the prayers that were lifted up in this way.' (End of Gary's report).

Oh Lord, send your fire into our hearts that we might spread it to our communities as we burn like bright lamps. Form us, like John the Baptist, into burning lights for your glory for

> *'John was a lamp that burned and gave light, and you chose*
> *for a time to enjoy his light.'*   (John 5:35)

Chapter 14

Ramping Up for Revival

'The out-pouring of the Spirit affects the reviving of the church, the awakening of the masses, and the movement of uninstructed peoples toward the Christian faith; the revived church, by many or by few, is moved to engage in evangelism, in teaching, and in social action.' [161]
(J. Edwin Orr)

Today there is so much to say about revival that I scarcely know where to begin. The earth is in a season of revival, stoked with sacred fire. While revival continues to rage in Pensacola and Buenos Aires, other places such as Salem and Portland, Oregon; Irian Jaya, Indonesia; Brisbane, Melbourne and Sydney, Australia are also hot spots. Read this report from the Christian Life Centre Mount Annan in Sydney,

> 'We are a church committed to revival for ourselves and for our nation. Sunday September 28, 1997 started out as any other service; with around 500 people celebrating God, with strong and exuberant praise and worship rounded off by singing 'Love You So Much' ... and that's where everything changed. Suddenly the Presence of God flooded the room to such an extent that it became difficult to breathe. The fear of God swept over every person as a Spirit of Judgement and Burning fell upon all believers and began to take our breath away. Senior Pastor Adrian Gray, called every person to instantly obey the Holy Spirit, without question, and

come to the altar to present themselves to God. Every person without exception ran to the front, afraid to do anything but obey. The Fire of God began to burn away every unclean thing in the lives of His people. This intensified so much that you could actually smell burning in the room. People who are not known for displays of emotion were overcome by the Fear of God, weeping and repenting as God began to show them the state of their own souls ... The Fire of God intensified, beginning to totally overwhelm many as they fell to the floor devoid of strength ... Most were weeping uncontrollably, while many stood awestruck before the Lord.'

I believe that God will saturate many churches of the 21st century with His presence and power – not unlike the one above. They will become revived churches marked by the fear of God and holiness. While the distinctive of renewal is **fun** in God for healing and commitment. The distinctive of revival is the **fear** of God for holiness and consecration. The church needs reviving. What follows is only the tip of the iceberg,

'Researchers have discovered that 3,500 people leave the church every day in the United States. According to studies by the Association of Church Missions Committees (ACMC), 250,000 of the 300,000 US Protestant congregations are either stagnant or dying. Research on church growth in the US in the 1980s uncovered disturbing statistics: 85 percent of churches were losing members during the 80s, while, 14 percent grew only by transfer growth. Only 1 percent actually recorded growth by conversions. According to Peter Wagner, during the 1980s not a single county in the United States had a net growth in church attendance.' [162]

Why do so many people not want to join or stay in our churches? Why are our churches not forces in the hand of almighty God? Is it because we often hole up in our Christian huddles to preach, pray, and build programs for ourselves? Is it because we have passion for community but little passion for cause? Is it because we tolerate the cancers of disunity and compromise that ravage our vital organs? Is it because we search for man-made techniques of church growth and management rather than search for God's empowering Presence? We need revived churches. How do we know when our church is in need of revival? Charles Finney suggests seven signs,

1. When there is a lack of brotherly love and confidence among those who profess to be Christians.
2. When there are dissensions, jealousies, and backbiting among those who profess Christianity.
3. When there is a worldly spirit in the church.
4. When church members fall into gross and scandalous sin.
5. When there is a spirit of controversy in the church or in the land.
6. When the wicked triumph over the church and revile it.
7. When sinners are careless and stupid and sinking into hell unconcerned, it is time for the church to stir itself.[163]

We need **prepared and praying hearts** now that respond to Hosea's plea:

> 'Sow for yourselves righteousness; reap in mercy; break up your fallow ground, for it is time to seek the LORD, till He comes and rains righteousness on you.' (Hosea 10:12 NKJV)

What is Revival?

Revival is not evangelistic campaigns or special camp meetings. Revival is a sovereign and 'surprising work of God' that brings life back to believers, awakens unbelievers to that new life, and transforms churches and communities. In the Welsh Revival of 1904, Evan Roberts often prayed, 'Bend the church and save the people.' Revival is 'heaven upon earth.' The word revival comes from the Latin *revivere* meaning 'to live again.' Repentance, forgiveness, and refreshing from the Lord characterize biblical revival. As Peter advised,

> 'Repent, then, and turn to God, so that your sins may be wiped out, that times of refreshing may come from the Lord.' (Acts 3:19)

'Revival is to be understood as an unusual manifestation of the power of the grace of God in convincing and converting careless sinners, and in quickening and increasing the faith and piety of believers.' [164]

In revival, God takes the initiative as He comes suddenly, dramatically, and precisely to a prepared and praying people. Of the Welsh Revival someone reported that 'The outpouring of the Spirit came dramatically with precision, in the second week in November, 1904, on the same day – both in the north and in the south.' [165] Revival came to Pensacola precisely on June 18, 1995. Revival can't be 'worked up' from earth through man's efforts. It can only 'come down' from heaven through God's efforts. The Psalmist prayed, *'Part your heavens, O LORD, and come down'* (Psalm 144:5). The Lord announced to Habbakuk,

> *'Look among the nations and watch – be utterly astounded! For I will work a work in your days which you would not believe, though it were told you.'*   (Habbakuk 1:5, NKJV)

As evangelical churches, how do we ramp up for revival? Let me suggest a few principles from Scripture and history.

Pray for Revival

Revivals bear the characteristics and results of Pentecost where *'They all joined together constantly in prayer,'* (Acts 1:14) and *'When the day of Pentecost came, they were all together in one place. Suddenly a sound like the blowing of a violent wind came from heaven and filled the whole house where they were sitting'* (Acts 2:1–2). J. Edwin Orr, an expert on revival, borrowing from Matthew Henry, declared that 'Whenever God is ready to do something new with his people, he always sets them to praying.' Do you know of any revival that started without unified prayer? They begin and continue in unified prayer. Unified prayer can shake our churches and communities with the Holy Spirit. In Acts 4:31–32 Luke reports that,

> *'After they prayed, the place where they were meeting was shaken. And they were all filled with the Holy Spirit and*

spoke the word of God boldly. All the believers were one in heart and mind.'

Brian Edwards gives an example where this literally occurred,

> 'An example of this happened at Arnol on the Isle of Lewis in the 1940s. Towards the close of the prayer meeting in the home of an elder, the local blacksmith was asked to pray. His prayer turned to the promises of God and to his own thirst for God and concluded: "O God, your honour is at stake, and I now challenge you to fulfil your covenant engagement and do what you have promised to do." At that moment the house shook and "Dishes rattled in the sideboard, as wave after wave of Divine power swept through the house." When this group of praying people closed the prayer meeting and went outside, they found "the community alive with an awareness of God."' [166]

In 1857, Jeremiah Lanphier, a New York businessman turned missionary, advertised a weekly Wednesday noon-hour prayer meeting at the Dutch Church on the corner of Fulton Street, New York City. After waiting thirty minutes at the first meeting, six people finally arrived. Next week twenty came. In October, they decided to have daily prayer meetings. Within six months 10,000 businessmen met daily to pray for revival. Within two years one million Americans came into the Kingdom with the same amount in Great Britain. [167]

At the turn of the century, Seth Joshua, an evangelist and early leader in the Welsh Revival of 1904, 'felt a danger of the prevailing emphasis upon educational rather than spiritual attainments ... had it laid upon his heart to pray God to go and take a lad from the coal-mine or from the field, even as He took Elisha from the plough, to revive His work.' [168] God answered that prayer with a twenty-six-year-old former coal-miner and blacksmith named Evan Roberts. Evan Roberts prayed for thirteen years that God would send revival to Wales. For three months in the Spring of 1904, God gave him a vision for 100,000 souls. It took God only eight months – from October 31, 1904 till June, 1905 – to reach the goal. In spite of leakage to mission halls and overseas emigration, by 1914, 80,000 converts were still in the membership of the Welsh churches.[169] J. Edwin Orr notes, 'The meetings consisted almost entirely by prayer and praise and were under the direct control of the Spirit of God.'[170]

The Pentecostal revival of 1906–09, with daily meetings held in a run-down Methodist church on 312 Azusa Street in Los Angeles, started elsewhere. They started a few miles away in prayer meetings led by William J. Seymour at the home of Richard and Ruth Asberry, at 214 Bonnie Brae Street. The Holy Spirit fell there on April 9, 1906. I have visited the actual restored Pentecostal heritage house. In 1905, reports of the Welsh revival stirred local prayer meetings and revivals in the Los Angeles area. So many people crammed into the prayer meetings on Bonnie Brae street that they moved them to Azusa street.

Frank Bartleman, an early leader in the Pentecostal revival, 'corresponded with Evan Roberts in Wales asking him to pray for revival in Los Angeles, and he received answers in June, August, and November [1905] confirming that prayers were being offered on behalf of the saints in Los Angeles. Of course people were praying fervently in many quarters of Los Angeles as well.'[171]

Bartleman reported that in the beginning of the revival there was no platform or pulpit and that William Seymour, the 'nominal' leader, generally sat behind two empty shoe boxes, one on top of the other with his head in inside the top one during the meeting, in prayer ... The whole place was steeped in prayer ... The shekinah glory rested there.'[172] People underestimate or disallow the impact of this revival that began at a home prayer meeting. However,

> 'The early Pentecostal revival came as one of the greatest revivals of the modern period, perhaps almost as import-ant in its effects as the Protestant Reformation of the sixteenth century. Originating within the milieu of the Holiness movement of the late nineteenth century, it brought into existence hundreds of ecclesiastical

bodies and denominations worldwide, many of which quickly became some of the fastest growing religious organizations in the world.' [173]

There's another Pentecostal revival taking place today. On Father's Day, June 18, 1995, God unleashed His Spirit during the Sunday morning service at the Brownsville Assembly of God Church in Pensacola, Florida. Stephen Hill, the visiting speaker, preached on Psalm 77:11–12 and then gave altar calls for salvation, for those who had wandered away from the Lord, and for those who wanted a fresh touch from God. One thousand people responded.[174] Since that altar call, by late April 1998, over 133,000 people have come forward for salvation on the Wednesday through Saturday night meetings. How did it begin? With prayer. Over a period of $2\frac{1}{2}$ years, Pastor John Kilpatrick built his church into a house of prayer. In spite of his fears that few would continue to come, he dedicated the weekly Sunday evening services to revival prayer. Pastor Kilpatrick describes the June 18 Sunday this way,

> 'There was no question in my mind that prayer was as central to the revival itself as it was to the preparation of it ... When Steve got up to preach, he could hardly get through his sermon, he was so excited about the altar call. He kept telling us, "Folks, God is going to move this morning. God is going to move this morning..." Yes, we had been praying for two-and-a-half years that God would bring revival; but I wondered if He really would ... [During the altar call] I walked off the right side of the platform with Steve to help him pray for people, but I began to feel a little strange standing next to him as he prayed ... Suddenly, I felt a wind blow through my legs, just like in the second chapter of the book of Acts ... and suddenly both my ankles flipped over so that I could hardly stand. [Later] I took the microphone and shouted, "Folks, this is it. The Lord is here. Get in, get in." I realized God had indeed come, that He had answered our prayers for revival. The **feast of fire** had begun!' [175]

R.E. Davies remarks that 'The most constant of all factors which appear in revivals is that of **urgent**, **persistent**, **prayer**. This fact is acknowledged by all writers on the subject. Such prayer is both part of the preparation for revival, and also a characteristic of churches and Christians who are revived.'[176] Prayer births and maintains revival. Repentance is not far behind.

Embrace Ruthless Repentance

I know of no biblical or historical revival that lacked repentance. Repentance precedes revival and is a condition for it (2 Chronicles 7:14). 'Repentance is a **gift** from God. Without it, sinners cannot be regenerated and saints cannot be renewed. **Repentance is God's activating grace**. It remakes and restores and repairs ... Repentance is the most basic of basics, the very first of the elementary teachings of Christ (see Hebrews 6:1).'[177] Biblical repentance is,

> 'A turning away from sin, disobedience, or rebellion and a turning back to God (Matthew 9:13; Luke 5:32). In a more general sense, repentance means a change of mind (Genesis 6:6–7) or a feeling of remorse or regret for past conduct (Matthew 27:3). True repentance is a "godly sorrow" for sin, an act of turning around and going in the opposite direction. This type of repentance leads to a fundamental change in a person's relationship to God. In Jesus' preaching of the kingdom of God is seen the truth that repentance and faith are two sides of the same coin: by repentance, one turns away from sin; by faith, one turns toward God in accepting the Lord Jesus Christ.'[178]

Repentance is a central message of the New Testament (Matthew 3:8; Mark 1:15; Acts 3:19–20; 2 Corinthians 7:8–10; James 4:8–10). The phrase 'return to the Lord' was also a central message about repentance in the Old Testament (Deuteronomy 4:30; 2 Chronicles 30:6–8; Jeremiah 3:22; Lamentations 3:40; Hosea 6:1–2). Repentance is key for those who have little awareness of God's presence. Brian Edwards writes,

'The reason there is so little repentance among our congregations today is not just that our sermons are not directed against sin, but that God is not felt among us. Those who know themselves to be in the presence of a holy God are always aware of personal sin.' [179]

Repentance means we will regularly humble ourselves. I've had to on several occasions. In the Spring of 1997 we felt the Lord convict our leadership team of sins we had historically committed in twelve major areas. Through many intercessory people, we developed a statement in those twelve areas to acknowledge and repent of and then twelve opposite areas to affirm and declare. As pastors and elders we went before the whole church during the Sunday morning service as I read out the declarations. The people applauded. It had a dramatic effect in the church and in our hearts. We must embrace ruthless repentance at three levels: personal, identificational, and corporate.

1. Personal repentance

Like Charlie Brown says, 'Everyone wants to change humanity but no one wants to change himself.' Repentance begins with you and me. Many revival reports show personal repentance as sudden, comprehensive, and deep. Of personal repentance in New England during the First Great Awakening, Jonathan Edwards records that,

'God has also seemed to have gone out of his usual way, in the **quickness** of his work, and the swift progress his Spirit has made in his operations on the hearts of many. It is wonderful that persons should be so **suddenly** and yet so **greatly** changed. Many have been taken from a loose and careless way of living, and seized with strong convictions of their guilt and misery, and in a very little time old things have passed away, and all things have become new with them.' [180]

May we pray the following,

'Search me, O God, and know my heart; try me, and know my anxieties; And see if there is any wicked way in me, and lead me in the way everlasting.' (Psalm 139:23–24 NKJV)

Again, in the fall of 1997, I felt to go before the church on a Sunday morning to repent of our and **my** approach to fund-raising and lack of faith concerning finances. It had a good effect in the church. One person remarked, 'Gee, if the pastors come before us in humility and repentance where does that leave the rest of us?' Evan Roberts trumpeted, 'God cannot do a great work through you until he does a great work in you.' We will have revived churches as we invite God to do a great work in **us** first.

2. Corporate repentance

Corporate repentance occurs when a church, a group, a community, or a nation comes before the Lord to confess their collective guilt (see Joel 2:12–19 and Jonah 3–4). Groups of people can sin and repent as can individuals. C. Peter Wagner remarks that 'Wherever many individuals are meaningfully linked together in a social network, that group can sin, not as individuals, but **as a group**. When it does, each individual member of the group is, to one degree or another, identified with the corporate sin whether the person personally participated in the act itself or not.'[181]

Around the world, groups are engaging in some intense corporate repentance. This is happening in *Promise Keepers* events where thousands of men repent of their racism or denominationalism. It's happening in the many '40 Days of Fasting and Prayer' initiatives originally spear-headed in 1994 by Bill Bright, President of Campus Crusade for Christ. The famous text of 2 Chronicles 7:14 is a key basis for corporate repentance, where:

> *'If my people, who are called by my name, will humble themselves and pray and seek my face and turn from their wicked ways, then will I hear from heaven and will forgive their sin and will heal their land.'*

3. Identificational repentance

Identificational repentance is similar to corporate repentance except that an individual or a group can participate. It is where a person or group 'identifies' with past sins that individuals or groups committed, owns responsibility for them as if they themselves committed them and intercedes on their behalf to heal those wounds of the past in the present. Exodus 20:5 indicates that God *'punishes the children for the sin of the fathers to the third and fourth generation of those who hate me.'* Fathers can transmit their unrepentant sin to their children, grandchildren, and great grandchildren. There becomes collective and progressive guilt.

There are biblical examples of this. Daniel, in Babylon, fasted, prayed and identified in repentance with a former generation whose sin led Judah into seventy years of captivity.

> *'I prayed to the* LORD *my God and confessed: "O Lord, the great and awesome God, who keeps his covenant of love with all who love him and obey his commands, we have sinned and done wrong. We have been wicked and have rebelled; we have turned away from your commands and laws."'*
>
> (Daniel 9:4–5)

Nehemiah, in Persia, also fasted, prayed and identified in repentance with the returned exiles who left Jerusalem in shambles and disobeyed the Law of Moses,

> *'Let your ear be attentive and your eyes open to hear the prayer your servant is praying before you day and night for your servants, the people of Israel. I confess the sins we Israelites, including myself and my father's house, have committed against you. We have acted very wickedly toward you. We have not obeyed the commands, decrees and laws you gave your servant Moses.'* (Nehemiah 1:6–7)

John Dawson, author of *Taking Our Cities For God* and *Healing America's Wounds*[182] writes about identifying with the sins of the city and nation and engaging in identificational repentance. This is beginning to occur in a number of places. C. Peter Wagner reports,

> 'Japanese Christian leaders have gone to cities of Asia to repent of Japanese occupation in World War II. Brazilian leaders have repented to Paraguayans for a brutal war that involved not only appropriating land that was not theirs, but a bloody massacre as well. Germans have

gathered in Holland in repentance for atrocities of Hitler. New Zealanders have publicly admitted and confessed their abuse and their oppression of the native Maori people. Here in the United States, Lutherans have repented for the anti-Semitism found in Martin Luther's writings. Southern Baptists, at their national convention, took official action to apologize to African-Americans for endorsing slavery. Methodist leaders were among a group who repented on site of the sins of Col. John Chivington, a Methodist lay minister, who led the atrocious and shameful massacre of Arapaho and Cheyenne Indians at Sand Creek near Denver more than 100 years ago. Some months later, the United Methodist General Conference followed suit by passing a resolution denouncing their ancestor's actions and apologizing for the Sand Creek atrocity.'[183]

There are also obstacles to remove along the way.

Remove Obstacles to Revival

Laodicean Lukewarmness

A major obstacle of revival is what I call 'Laodicean Lukewarmness.' Like the Laodicean church of Revelation 3:14–21, it encompasses churches that have become materialistic, proud, self-sufficient, spiritually complacent and compromised. Laodicean churches are neither cold nor refreshing, or hot and literally 'zesty.' Rather they are lukewarm – literally, nauseatingly 'tepid.' They are indifferent, neutral, and irrelevant. These are churches whose outward wealth is spiritual poverty. Laodicea prided itself on its wealth, clothing trade, and eye-salve. The culture contaminated the church because the church became lukewarm. Of the messages to the seven churches in Revelation, 'Laodicea has the grim distinction of being the only Church of which the Risen Christ has nothing good to say.'[184]

The way out of Laodicean Lukewarmness is to repent and let Jesus back in the church for fellowship with him at the evening meal. The meal referenced in this passage was the evening meal, *deipnon* – the main meal of the day. It was no hurried meal where people could linger over after a day's work was done.[185] If churches will open their doors of access to the knocking Christ who is outside, He will come inside and linger long with them. Only then can revival come.

Scorning the sacred

In his book, *Let No One Deceive You*, Dr Michael Brown wrote a chapter entitled 'Scorning the Sacred: When the Critics Enter the Danger Zone.'[186] He builds his case around Mark 3:28–30 where Jesus warns that there's no forgiveness for those who blaspheme the Holy Spirit. He writes, 'To blaspheme the Spirit is to knowingly attribute to the devil Jesus' work done in the power of the Holy Spirit. Why tamper with a sin which can lead to eternal judgment? It is the ultimate offense ... **There is nothing more dangerous than blasphemy of the Spirit**.'[187]

We wouldn't say that anyone who opposes revival is guilty of blaspheming the Holy Spirit. There are well-meaning Christians who are so fearful, ignorant, or even deceived that they don't realize they are calling a genuine move of God a 'counterfeit.' All revivals have religious opponents who cannot or will not 'recognize the time of their visitation' (Luke 19:44). Instead they 'scorn the sacred,' and in actual effect enter the danger zone of blaspheming the Spirit. Better to reserve judgement and err on the side of grace than to boldly oppose, attack, or resist something with such spiritual magnitude. When we understand how grave blasphemy of the Spirit is, would we not be cautious to not do anything that even resembles it? We should be like the former alcoholic who will not go near a bar or liquor store.

It's OK to have honest caution while we, like the Bereans, have *'more noble character'* and *'receive the message with great eagerness and examine the Scriptures every day to see if what ... was said is true'* (Acts 17:11).

Religious spirit

The person with a 'religious spirit' talks, acts, and prays as if they are 'spiritual.' In reality they are 'religious.' They are like the Pharisees who meticulously observed religious laws and rituals and appeared to walk with God. The religious spirit is exacting, performance-based and graceless. It's a charlatan masquerading in 'clerical cleanliness' bound to rules rather than relationship, to pride rather than humility. It's hypocritical. A religious hypocrite,

1. Claims to have an exclusive corner on the truth, even among Gods' people.
2. Is self-righteous.
3. Is a slave to human praise and criticism.
4. Is jealous, envious, and competitive.
5. Is highly critical.
6. Wants his spirituality to be seen.
7. Is cynical and skeptical.
8. Produces bondage instead of freedom.
9. Is more concerned with outward forms and traditions than with the power of God, mercy, and compassion.
10. Is narrowly nationalistic and dangerously denominational.[188]

The religious spirit promotes what John Wesley called 'sour godliness.' He said that 'Sour godliness is the devil's religion. It does not owe its inception to truly spiritual people. I suspect that sour godliness originated among unhappy, semi-religious people who had just enough religion to make them miserable, but not enough to do them good.'[189]

Carnal resistance

Another obstacle to revival is carnal resistance. The Bible uses the term 'stiff-necked.' Ever used the phrase 'stubborn as a mule?' Ever seen someone try to guide a mule with a bit in its mouth? A mule will stiffen its neck with stubborn resistance. Rebellious and stiff-necked people are obstacles to revival. God often charged Israel with being 'stiff-necked.' Through carnal resistance they would not bend with God's laws and ways. From Acts 6:8–10, read the following account about Stephen,

> *'Now Stephen, a man full of God's grace and power, did great wonders and miraculous signs among the people. Opposition arose, however, from members of the Synagogue of the Freedmen (as it was called) – Jews of Cyrene and Alexandria*

as well as the provinces of Cilicia and Asia. These men began to argue with Stephen, but they could not stand up against his wisdom or the Spirit by whom he spoke.'

Stephen, a man full of God's grace and power addressed a Synagogue of religious people who opposed him. In Acts 7:51, he blasted them with,

'You stiff-necked people, with uncircumcised hearts and ears! You are just like your fathers: You always resist the Holy Spirit!'

Wouldn't you rather, as John Arnott suggests, deal with fleshy zeal than carnal resistance? God honors humble and pliable hearts that cry out like Evan Roberts, 'O Lord, bend me.'

Get in the Fire

We cannot stoke our own revival fires through human efforts or measures. We can locate them and do our best to get in them. As reports of revival spread, thousands make visits to such places as Toronto, Pensacola, Buenos Aires, and Sydney. When people enter the 'ethos' or 'hot house' environments of revival they often 'catch the fire' – an impartation. To get in the fire, we don't have to visit Pensacola or possibly can't make it. However, people did make pilgrimages to hear John the Baptist and then Jesus, and then to Jerusalem on the Day of Pentecost and later to places like Wales and Azusa Street. If you were there you would experience and catch something. If you weren't, you wouldn't. It's like inviting people to church – when they come they experience God. When they stay home they miss that experience.

I'm talking more about having hearts for not missing God, wherever and however he is moving. As Stephen Hill reminds us, 'The opportunity of a lifetime must be seized during the lifetime of the opportunity.' Seize the opportunity to get near the heat of revival fires while they continue to burn.

Before he came to Pensacola, Stephen Hill heard about the renewal in England. He made an appointment to see Sandy

Millar, Vicar of Holy Trinity Brompton (HTB) in London. Steve asked for prayer. As Sandy prayed for him, God gave Steve a fresh touch. He shared that experience with the Brownsville Assembly of God at that Father's Day service in June, 1995. The rest is church history! Do you see how the flame spreads? Eleanor Mumford of Southwest London Vineyard went to Toronto in 1994 and received a blessing. She shared her experience with the staff and people of HTB. We should pray that revival fire will come to wherever we are at, but let's also go to where the fires are already burning.

Go for Atomic Unity

In November 1996, Nancy Saura, one of our prophetic ladies received a brief word from the Lord. God simply gave her the words, 'Binary Confusion.' She researched the meaning of the words 'Binary *Fusion*,' and found the following: 'Binary fusion is the release of nuclear energy from the fusion of two separate parts. For this fusion to occur there must be a strong magnetic field and extremely high heat from an external heat source. Binary fusion releases seven times greater power than nuclear fission which occurs through splitting of the atom.'

As a group prayed for understanding, they felt the Lord spoke about the incredible power and anointing that will be released when the Body of Christ comes into **unity**. The strategy of Satan is to keep the church in binary **confusion** – separate parts in disarray and confusion. The magnetic field is the draw towards the centrality of Christ and the Cross – the only true basis of unity. Perhaps the intense heat required for fusion to occur is the circumstances the Lord allows in our lives to discipline and purify our faith and character.

If we do our part to ignite the unity of binary fusion we will become blessed people of the Presence, saturated with God. If we do our part to pray and model the prayer of Jesus in John 17, binary fusion will unleash atomic unity with explosive revival in our church and community. Then we will each confidently declare, 'Wow, I had a part as a pillar saint who helped build the fireplace and fanned the flame of a revived church for the 21st century.' Go for it!

Afterword

Ground Level Christians
for Revived Churches

*'The greatness of a person is in his humility before God not
in his eloquence before men.'*

My wife and I had finished an excellent Saturday evening
dinner at our home with our School of Leadership and
Church Renewal staff. As we ate, we talked of the school
and enjoyed laughter and friendship together. Later, we all
watched a live video-taped interview of an Estonian pastor
that one of our staff members filmed inside this pastor's
church. His name is Rein Uuemois. Our mood quickly
changed. We sat stunned as we listened to him recount
his story of revival, healing, and miracles that occurred
in his church services from 1975–1985. The church was
regularly jammed with Estonians, Russians and Ukrainians
who came long distances.

This humble Estonian pastor spoke with wonder in his
eyes and pain in his heart as he reflected on those profound
experiences. For a decade he helped lead a revival where
healing, genuine miracles and mass conversions broke loose
like a prairie flood – until the KGB shut it down. He also
spoke of people hauled off to concentration camps never
to return. As he told his story with humility, he honored
God's glory and grace while never showing bitterness –
disappointment yes, a broken heart yes, but vengeance and
bitterness, no.

Rein also planned to attend the last five weeks of our school! After I saw the video I remarked, 'And we are supposed to teach him something? Yeah, right! He should be teaching us!' His five weeks with us greatly impacted me and him as well – it was a divine appointment. What I saw was a model of the kind of revived Christian that God honors. People noted for brokenness and submission, who will, in the title of Bill Hybels' book, 'Descend Into Greatness.'

The Kingdom of Brokenness and Submission

The next morning I joined Richard Anderton, our Pastor of Children's Ministries, and his Kids Church leaders for breakfast to bless them. As each leader took a turn to share, his Kids Church supervisor broke down in tears as she expressed the repentance the Lord had brought her. The whole group felt the Lord was about to bring repentance to the children as well. Then a few hours later in the Sunday morning service I preached a heart message to our people on 1 Samuel 19 entitled, 'The Kingdom of Brokenness and Submission.' I showed the contrast between the natural (human) order of Saul and the spiritual (divine) order of David. Saul embodied rebellion, anger, fear, jealousy, and manipulation. This ultimately placed him in the sphere of witchcraft and demonic attacks (1 Samuel 15:22–23; 18:10; 19:10). Saul was not a broken and submissive man. God rejected him. In contrast, David embodied obedience, self-control, humility and courage. He was a broken and submissive man. God accepted him. Saul represented spiritual abuse while David represented spiritual use.

In my preparation that week, I re-read Gene Edward's book, *A Tale of Three Kings: A Study in Brokenness*. All Christians should read this. Below is a main point.

> 'What do I do when the kingdom I'm in is ruled by a spear-wielding king? ... What does a man do in the middle of a knife-throwing contest? ...
> The answer is, "You get stabbed to death."
> "What is the necessity of that? Or the good of it?"

You have your eyes on the wrong King Saul. As long as you look at your king, you will blame him, and him alone, for your present hell. Be careful, for God has **His** eyes fastened on another King Saul. Not the visible one standing up there throwing spears at you. No, God is looking at **another** King Saul. One just as bad – or worse. God is looking at the King Saul in you.

"In me?" . . .

You are King Saul.

He breathes in the lungs and beats in the breast of all of us. There is only one way to get rid of him. He must be annihilated.

David the sheepherder would have grown up to become King Saul II, except that God cut away the Saul inside David's heart. The operation, by the way, took years and was a brutalizing experience that almost killed the patient. And what were the scalpel that God used to remove this inner Saul? God used the outer Saul.' [190]

Ground Level Christians

God has been introducing me to the school of 'ground level leadership' – the place of brokenness, submission and humility. It began on April 3, 1995. That's when a little boy my wife was baby-sitting at our home died after jumping off our front retaining wall as he played with our two sons. We felt grief so deep words cannot describe. For the next three years, the journey 'down' continued as I began to get in touch with my weakness.

Through many situations, God put me in my place by granting me just and unjust criticism, a lack of public recognition and requests from people to do ministry, and a sense of feeling very unimportant, overlooked, and dispensable. I also became a lot more in touch with the struggles, pain, and weakness of others. Where I was too demanding and stern with others, God showed me a softer path of grace and understanding.

I became the 'point man' for our whole church as God led us into a long season where we had to lay things down, deal with our pride and disunity. In March 1998, during our

40-day season of prayer and fasting, God met us in our nothingness. At this same time, we were well into a preaching series on 'The Beatitudes' in Matthew 5. Through this biblical series, God reinforced where he was taking us and what we were experiencing – poverty in Spirit, mourning, meekness, and purity of heart through brokenness, submission, and humility. As Ralph Bromley put it, 'Roger, God is testing our steel.' God's hammering compelled me to search my motives as I logged time on my knees. In our descent to greatness we must embrace weakness and humility. As someone said, 'When God measures a man or woman, he puts the tape around their heart, not around their head.'

Brokenness means 'to be subdued totally; to be humbled, weakened and made submissive.' Submission means 'to yield or surrender (oneself) to the will or authority of another.' These are the kinds of Christians that God wants for the revived church. In a word, **humble** ones. The word 'humble' is from the Latin word *humilis* meaning 'low, on the ground.' *Humilis* is derived from *humus* – meaning 'the ground.' When we are broken and humble we are low – **ground level**. That's the place of submission. Of humility Jonathan Edwards writes,

> 'The eminently humble Christian is as it were clothed with lowliness, mildness, meekness, gentleness of spirit and behaviour, and with a soft, sweet, condescending winning air and deportment; these things are just like garments to him, he is clothed all over with them (1 Peter 5:5; Colossians 3:12) ... Pure Christian humility has no such thing as roughness, or contempt, or fierceness, or bitterness in its nature; it makes a person like a little child, harmless and innocent, that none need to be afraid of; or like a lamb, destitute of all bitterness, wrath, anger, and clamour; agreeable to Ephesians 4:31.'[191]

The key to pure spiritual power is humility. As Jim Cymbala declares: '**God is attracted to weakness**. He can't resist those who humbly and honestly admit how desperately they need him.'[192] The Bible declares,

> *'Humility and the fear of the* Lord *bring wealth and honor and life.'* (Proverbs 22:4)

As in Saul's case, we can be filled with the Spirit and still be no good. We can look for God's power but not His presence. We can seek His hand and not His face. **God doesn't build revived churches with powerful people, He builds them with pure people**. Again, Gene Edwards,

> 'Remember: God sometimes gives power to men for unseen reasons. A man can be living in the grossest of sin and the outward gift will still be working perfectly...
>
> What does this world need: gifted men, outwardly empowered? Or broken men, inwardly transformed?
>
> Keep in mind that some of the men who have been given the very power of God have raised armies, defeated the enemy, brought forth mighty works of God, preached and prophesied with unparalleled power and eloquence...
>
> And thrown spears,
> And hated other men,
> And attacked other men,
> And plotted to kill,
> And prophesied naked,
> And even consulted witches.'[193]

Appendix

Characteristics of Revivals and Awakenings

The following list of characteristics of revivals and awakenings was compiled by Richard M. Riss, author of *A Survey of 20th Century Revival Movements in North America* and *Images of Revival.*[194] Not all revivals will display all these characteristics but all revivals will display many or most of them.

1. How Awakenings Arise
a. They always emerge against a backdrop of very serious spiritual decline or intense spiritual dryness.
b. They are the product of intense prayer.
c. When people pray for re-awakening, God seems to give the answer to their prayers in places that they least expect it.
d. At the beginning of an awakening, there is often an exhilarating sense of expectancy.
e. Revivals are often brought about by telling people about the revivals of the past.
f. There is often a specific point in time at the outset of an outpouring of the Holy spirit at which God's presence is suddenly recognized by the people. The power of God falls spontaneously.
g. Revivals of this kind seem to emerge at the same time in many different places.

2. Who Becomes Involved?
a. The Lord breathes new life into the Church.
b. He brings multitudes of new believers into His body.
c. Those who are already Christians enter more deeply into the fullness of salvation.

d. People recognize a similarity of the revival to any previous revivals they have experienced.
e. Backsliders are reclaimed.
f. People often come out of curiosity or skepticism and become believers.
g. There are conversions of ministers.

3. The Spread of the News
a. At the outset of revival, there is very little organization.
b. Advertising is largely by word of mouth.
c. People are sometimes drawn to the scene of revival by an irresistible power.
d. People come from miles away.
e. People flock from everywhere.
f. There are crowds.
g. It is contagious.
h. There are often secular newspaper accounts of an awakening.

4. Conviction of Sin, Righteousness, and Judgment
a. Revival is characterized by widespread repentance and brokenness.
b. There is a great deal of meditation upon God's character.
c. There is an awakening of conscience.
d. There is conviction of sin.
e. People are given an immediate revelation of God's glory and of their own sinfulness and inadequacy before Him.
f. In some cases, people for blocks around are confronted with their own sin and God's majesty.
g. People suddenly become deeply convinced of their lostness.
h. An awesome fear of God and His judgment comes upon everyone.
i. Revivals bring the individual face to face with the eternal questions of one's nature and destiny.
j. People suddenly become aware of the terrors of hell.
k. This is accompanied by deep distress over one's wickedness.
l. The urge to pray, especially for salvation, is irresistible.
m. There are sometimes manifestations of shaking or trembling.

n. There are often strange manifestations of emotion in people in response to these experiences, including laughter, weeping, barking or yelping, and roaring.

o. People therefore seek forgiveness from God through Christ's shed blood.

p. They then find redemption in His blood; they are given assurance of forgiveness of sin and of salvation.

q. This is accompanied with joy and peace.

r. Even the sceptical and stubborn will also grieve over their sins until they find assurance.

5. Freedom and Reconciliation

a. God frees people from bondage to sinful habits, bad attitudes, and emotional disturbances, breaking the power of 'canceled sin,' as Charles Wesley put it.

b. Old prejudices are changed radically.

c. Broken homes are reunited.

d. There is widespread reconciliation.

e. There comes a depth of love for one's brothers and sisters in Christ beyond measure.

f. People receive a fresh sense of the unity of believers in all times and places.

g. It puts an end to cursing, blasphemy, drunkenness and uncleanness in a town. There is a cessation of fighting, clamor, bitterness, and so forth.

h. Rather, joy and peace become predominant in a place that has experienced an awakening.

6. Heaven Upon Earth

a. People become so preoccupied with the things of God that they don't want to talk about anything else.

b. There is an unusually vivid sense of God's presence, and of joy, love and peace.

c. There are sometimes manifestations of laughter and speechlessness.

d. There is a completely different, refreshing atmosphere where God is present.

e. People experience heaven upon earth.

f. Meetings are often of protracted length. Time passes very quickly.

g. There is a feeling of release, or freedom in the Spirit.

h. People feel refreshed. There is a new lilt to everyone's steps.
i. People suddenly have an intense enthusiasm about the things of God.
j. There is considerable praise to God.
k. There is singing in the Spirit of such harmonies as are almost never heard on earth.
l. There is dancing in the Spirit. There are manifestations of spiritual gifts.
m. Children prophesy.

7. Ministry During Divine Visitations

a. God often raises up people as instruments for bringing about revival who have few natural talents and abilities.
b. Women and lay people find a greater place for leadership in revival.
c. His Word goes forth in power.
d. The Lord anoints with the Spirit the preaching, teaching, counseling, and music such that it has an ability to penetrate the hearts of the people.
e. There is always considerable revelation upon God's Word, which takes on a new freshness.
f. People in a revival are almost invariably orthodox theologically on the great basics of the Christian faith. There is a great emphasis upon the Bible and its teachings.
g. There is a great stress usually laid upon the suffering, cross, blood and death of Jesus Christ.
h. People fall under God's power.
i. People begin to laugh or cry, or develop characteristics similar to drunkenness.
j. Physical ailments are sometimes healed.
k. These phenomena are accompanied by the healing of shattered lives.

8. Enthusiasm for God's Precious Word

a. The Bible comes alive for people
b. There is always a deep thirst for the Word of God.
c. People hang upon every word that is preached.
d. There are phenomenal increases in the sales of New Testaments and Bibles.

e. Those who are used of God in bringing about revival receive far more calls to preach than they can ever answer, and are harried mercilessly.

9. Beyond Superficialities

a. A spirit of sacrifice is often prevalent in a revival.
b. People spend whole nights in prayer.
c. Revival usually produces a zeal for the saving of the lost and, there, for missions.
d. God brings revelation.
e. People gather together to share in the faith for mutual upbuilding.
f. Superficial profession, baptism and church membership pale into significance, with an emphasis being placed upon spiritual life, of which the former things are merely tokens.
g. Old institutional forms often begin to seem inadequate to people who are experiencing an awakening.

10. The Rise of Impurities

a. Human frailty is inevitably an ingredient in any revival.
b. It is case for amazement even to seasoned preachers and evangelists to see what happens during seasons of awakening.
c. Belief in the imminent coming of Christ has characterized every movement of awakening since the first century. This has often led to the setting of dates for Christ's return.
d. Those who try to mold a revival to their own tastes or control it are usually swept aside.
e. Because so many young, inexperienced converts are involved, there will be many extravagances.
f. There is a temptation to spiritual pride, and to take one's own imagination for impressions from God.
g. In a revival, there will always be some who violate biblical truth.
h. Belief that they alone are instrumental in the accomplishment of God's purposes often characterizes both individuals and groups experiencing revival.

11. Controversy During Outpourings of God's Spirit

a. There are always bad reports about what goes on in a revival, both true and false.

b. Many people remain aloof for this reason.

c. A revival is always accompanied with a great deal of controversy.

d. There is always intense opposition and persecution.

e. There is reproach upon every revival.

f. Revival always involves an advance of God's kingdom in spiritual warfare against the strongholds of Satan.

g. The enemy will attempt to hinder the work of God at all costs.

h. Satan attempts to discredit revival by mimicking God's work.

12. The Decline of an Awakening

a. A revival will crest to a high point and then decrease.

b. After a revival crests, offenses will come.

c. Many people will feel ill-will instead of good-will toward the leaders of a revival.

d. They will begin to disapprove of what they formerly approved.

e. They will fasten upon bad reports, true or false, in order to justify their changes in attitude.

f. Many of those who were more or less convinced will be afraid or ashamed to acknowledge their conviction of faith.

13. The Long-Term Effects

a. A new flood of hymns and scriptures set to music gains widespread circulation and use.

b. It has lasting, profound effects upon the lives of many of the people involved.

c. It spawns great ministries, which then thrive well past the time of the revival.

d. There is a tremendous impact on society and many social reforms are effected.

References

1. Charles Ludwig, *Francis Asbury: God's Circuit Rider*, Mott Media, 1984, p. 1.
2. Charles Hummel, *Fire in the Fireplace: Charismatic Renewal in the Nineties*, InterVarsity Press, 1993, p. 20.
3. Jimmy Long, *Generating Hope*, InterVarsity Press, 1997, p. 27.
4   Leith Anderson, *A Church for the 21st Century*, Bethany House Publishers, 1992, p. 16.
5. For several of the ideas and sources presented in the next few paragraphs, I am indebted to Pastor David Kalamen's teaching notes for his 'Christianity: Beyond 2000' seminar presented at Kelowna Christian Center, February 27–March 3, 1998.
6. Jimmy Long, op. cit., p. 61.
7. Faith Popcorn, *The Popcorn Report*, HarperBusiness, 1992, p. 12.
8. Faith Popcorn, *Clicking*, HarperBusiness, 1997, pp. 105–107.
9. Ibid., p. 114.
10. Ibid., p. 112 (italics mine).
11. Mike Starkey, *God, Sex, & Generation X*, Triangle, 1997, p. 5.
12 William M. Easum and Thomas G. Bandy, *Growing Spiritual Redwoods*, Abingdon Press, 1997, pp. 111–113.
13. James A. Belasco, *Teaching the Elephant to Dance*, Plume Books, 1991, p. 2.
14. Stephen R. Covey, *First Things First*, Simon & Schuster, 1994, p. 189.
15. Charles Hummel, op. cit., p. 20.
16. As cited by Jimmy Long, op. cit., p. 26.
17. David Bryant, *The Hope at Hand*, Baker Books, 1995, pp. 23–24.
18. Bill Bright, *The Coming Revival*, NewLife Publications, 1995, p. 34.
19. Op. cit., p. 65.

20. Bryant, op. cit., pp. 22–23.
21. Gene Getz, *Sharpening the Focus of the Church*, Victor Books, 1984; Frank Tillapaugh, *Unleashing the Church*, Regal Books, 1982.
22. For a detailed account, see Roger Helland, *Let the River Flow: Welcoming Renewal Into Your Church*, HarperCollins, 1996 and Bridge – Logos, 1996, Chapter 1. Also see, Wesley Campbell, *Welcoming a Visitation of the Holy Spirit*, Creation House, 1996, Chapter 4.
23. A very helpful source discussing the need for and difference between pioneers and homesteaders can be found in John Wimber's *Vineyard Reflections* issued in October/November/December 1993. Another helpful issue is the January/February 1994 one on 'A Leadership Shopping List.'
24. Margaret M. Poloma, *The Assemblies of God at the Crossroads: Charisma and Institutional Dilemmas*, The University of Tennessee Press, 1989, p. 21.
25. Clark H. Pinnock, *Flame of Love: A Theology of the Holy Spirit*, InterVarsity Press, 1996, p. 140.
26. Rick Warren, *The Purpose Driven Church*, Zondervan, 1995, pp. 121–22.
27. The following chart and discussion was adapted from John Wimber, 'The Church Growth Change Agent' in *Leadership and the Kingdom of God*, Seminar Notes, Vineyard Ministries International, 1986, p. 4.
28. See William Bridges, *Managing Transitions: Making the Most of Change*, Addison-Wesley Publishing Co., 1991.
29. Leith Anderson, *A Church for the 21st Century*, Bethany House Publishers, 1992, p. 62.
30. Ibid., pp. 63–64.
31. Pinnock, ibid., p. 171.
32. Ray S. Anderson, *Ministry on the Fireline: A Practical Theology for an Empowered Church*, InterVarsity Press, 1993, pp. 14–15.
33. Ibid., p. 14.
34. F.F. Bruce, *NIGTC Commentary on Galatians*, William B. Eerdmans Publishing, 1982, p. 257.
35. Clark Pinnock, op. cit., pp. 145–46.
36. This paragraph and the following chart was adapted from Jim Goll, *Prophetic Maturation*, Study Notes, Ministry to the Nations, 1996, p. 64.
37. Zeb Bradford Long and Douglas McMurry, *Receiving the Power*, Chosen Books, 1996, p. 82.

38 These and other references can be found in the above book, pp. 83–85.

39 James D.G. Dunn, *Jesus and the Spirit*, SCM Press, 1975, p. 54.

40 Ibid., p. 87.

41 Jim Goll, op. cit., p. 41.

42 Don Williams, 'Exorcising the Ghost of Newton,' in *Power Encounters*, ed. Kevin Springer, Harper & Row, 1988, p. 118.

43 M. Scott Peck, *The Different Drum*, New York: Simon & Schuster, 1987, p. 99.

44 For a fascinating application of quantum physics to organizational leadership, see Margaret J. Wheatley, *Leadership and the New Science: Learning About Organization From an Orderly Universe*, Berrett-Koehler Publishers, 1992, 1994.

45 Margaret J. Wheatley and Myron Kellner-Rogers, *A Simpler Way*, Berrett-Koehler Publishers, 1996.

46 Ibid., pp. 41, 57.

47 Ibid., pp. 58, 61.

48 Ibid., p. 66–7.

49 Ibid., p. 75.

50 Pinnock, op. cit., pp. 138–140.

51 The bulk of this chapter was adapted from Roger Helland, 'From Vision to Vehicle: Putting Wheels on Your Ideas for Ministry,' in *Equipping the Saints*, First Qtr. 1995 (used by permission).

52 Stephen R. Covey, A. Roger Merrill, Rebecca R. Merrill, *First Things First*, Simon & Schuster, 1994, p. 103–4, italics mine.

53 Laurie Beth Jones, *The Path*, Hyperion, 1996, p. 94.

54 John C. Maxwell, *Developing the Leader Within You*, Thomas Nelson Publishers, 1993, p. 153.

55 David Bryant, *The Hope at Hand*, Baker Books, 1995, p. 160.

56 Ibid., pp. 161–66.

57 Roger Helland, *Let the River Flow: Welcoming Renewal Into Your Church*, HarperCollins, 1996, Bridge-Logos, 1996.

58 Richard Foster, *Celebration of Discipline*, Revised Edition, Harper & Row, 1978, 1988, p. 8.

59 Jonathan Edwards, 'Revival of Religion in Northampton in 1740–42' in *Jonathan Edwards on Revival*, The Banner of Truth Trust, 1984, 1987, p. 159.

60 Brian H. Edwards, *Revival: A People Saturated With God*, Evangelical Press, pp. 73–74, 78–79.

61 Frank Bartleman, *Azusa Street*, Logos, 1980, p. 58.

62 See Randy Clark, *God Can Use Little Ole Me*, Destiny Image, 1998.

63 R. Paul Stevens and Phil Collins, *The Equipping Pastor*, The Alban Institute, 1993, p. 46.

64. Ibid, p. 41.

65. Ibid, p. 128.

66. Carl George and Robert Logan, *Leading & Managing Your Church*, Fleming H. Revell, 1987, p. 109.

67. Denny Gunderson, *Through the Dust*, YWAM Publishing, 1992, p. 27.

68. Ibid., p. 115.

69. John Wimber, *Power Evangelism*, Harper & Row, 1986, p. 107.

70. Ibid., p. 110.

71. Dieter Zander, 'The Gospel for Generation X: Making Room in the Church for "Busters,"' in *Leadership Magazine*, Spring 1995, p. 38.

72. Ibid.

73. As cited in Jimmy Long, *Generating Hope*, InterVarsity Press, 1997, p. 56.

74. Os Guiness, *Fit Bodies, Fat Minds*, Baker Book House, 1994, p. 128.

75. Jimmy Long, op. cit., p. 76.

76. Ibid., p. 39.

77. Ibid.

78. Ibid., p. 8.

79. As found in surveys by George Barna, *Generation Next*, Regal Books, 1995, p. 77 and Thom S. Ranier, *The Bridger Generation*, Broadman & Holman Publishers, 1997, p. 166.

80. Jimmy Long, op. cit., p. 35.

81. The following sub-titles and some of the content were adapted from Dieter Zander, op. cit., pp. 40–41. He is addressing the Gen X youth. However, Generation X, for many people, would constitute a blend of the characteristics of both the Busters and Bridgers. I believe there are similarities yet remarkable differences. However, I will blend them together within the following four points.

82. As reported in *Christianity Today*, February 3, 1997, p. 25.

83. Jonathan Edwards, 'Revival of Religion in Northampton in 1740–42' in *Jonathan Edwards on Revival*, The Banner of Truth Trust, 1984, 1987, p. 149.

84. Rick Warren, *The Purpose Driven Church*, Zondervan, 1995.

85. Ibid., p. 49.

86. An interview with Rick Warren, 'Comprehensive Health Plan,' *Leadership Magazine*, Summer 1997, p. 24.

87. Harry Blamires, *The Christian Mind: How Should a Christian Think?*, Servant Books, 1978, p. 3.

88. C. Peter Wagner, *Spreading the Fire*, Regal Books, 1994, p. 159.

89. Don Williams, 'Exorcising the Ghost of Newton' in *Power Encounters*, ed. Kevin Springer, Harper & Row, 1988, p. 125–26.
90. This chapter is adapted from Roger Helland, 'Wrestling With Worship,' in *Worship Update*, Vol. VI, Number 2.
91. Leith Anderson, *A Church for the 21st Century*, Bethany House Publishers, 1992, pp. 145–48.
92. Two of the best books I've come across that are informational and practical in the area of music and worship are: Bob Sorge, *Exploring Worship: A Practical Guide to Praise and Worship*, Self-published, 1987; and Donald P. Hustad, *Jubilate II: Church Music in Worship and Renewal*, Hope Publishing Co., 1981, 1993. Another more extensive treatment is the seven volume series edited by Robert E. Webber, *The Complete Guide of Christian Worship*, Star Song Publishing Group, 1993, 1994.
93. As written by Wesley in his *Journal* (September 8, 1784), from John Wesley, *The Works of John Wesley*, 3rd edn, Vol. IV, Hendrickson Publishers, 1872, reprint, 1984, p. 288.
94. David Bryant, 'God is Up to Something,' in *Pray!*, Premier Issue, 1997, p. 14.
95. Ibid.
96. Ibid, p. 122 citing Glen Martin and Dian Ginter, *Power House: A Step-by-Step Guide to Building a Church That Prays*, Broadman & Holman, 1994, p. 17.
97. C. Peter Wagner, *Churches That Pray*, Regal Books, 1993, p. 23.
98. George Barna, *User Friendly Churches*, Regal Books, 1991, p. 119.
99. Ibid., p. 120.
100. C. Peter Wagner, *Praying With Power*, Regal Books, 1997, p. 129 citing Thom Rainer, *Effective Evangelistic Churches*, Broadman & Holman Publishers, 1996, p. 67, (italics his).
101. C. Peter Wagner, *Churches That Pray*, Regal Books, 1993.
102. Ibid., p. 57.
103. Eifion Evans, *The Welsh Revival of 1904*, Evangelical Press of Wales, 1969, p. 72.
104. Wagner, *Praying With Power*, op. cit., p. 121, citing Carl Lawrence with David Wang, *The Coming Influence of China*, Vision House Publishing, 1996, p. 52.
105. Arthur Wallis, *In the Day of Thy Power*, Cityhill Publishing, Christian Literature Crusade, 1956, 1990, p. 159.
106. John Dawson, *Taking Our Cities for God*, Creation House, 1989.
107. Walter Wink, *Engaging the Powers*, Fortress Press, 1992, p. 299.
108. As reported in *Charisma Magazine*, March 1997, p. 22.
109. Leith Anderson, *A Church for the 21st Century*, Bethany House Publishers, 1992, p. 20.

110. Bob Sorge, *Exploring Worship*, Self-published, 1987, p. 33.

111. Brian H. Edwards, *Revival: A People Saturated With God*, Evangelical Press, 1990, pp. 134–36.

112. Ibid., p. 136.

113. Warren Wiersbe, *Real Worship*, Oliver Nelson, 1986, p. 130, citing Frank C. Senn, *Christian Worship in Its Cultural Setting*, Fortress Press, 1983, p. 75.

114. Ibid., p. 134.

115. James H. Rutz, *The Open Church*, The Seedsowers, 1992.

116. As published from the findings of Empty Tomb Inc. in *Leadership*, Spring 1998, p. 13.

117. Edwards, op. cit., p. 160.

118. Winkie Pratney, *Revival*, Whitaker House, 1983, 1984, p. 127, commenting on the preaching of revivalist Charles Finney, citing Miller, *Charles Finney*, cover.

119. George Sweeting, *Great Quotes and Illustrations*, Word Publishers, 1985, p. 219.

120. The two preceding sentences are borrowed from John Piper, *The Supremacy of God in Preaching*, Baker Book House 1990, pp. 84, 86.

121. Neil B. Wiseman, *The Untamed God*, Beacon Hill Press, 1997, p. 67.

122. Ibid., p. 70, citing Donald G. Miller, *The Way to Biblical Preaching*, Abingdon Press, 1957, p. 142.

123. Ibid., p. 75, citing a letter from John E. Riley, former president of Northwest Nazarene College.

124. Arthur Wallis, op. cit., pp. 83–84.

125. *George Whitefield's Journals*, The Banner of Truth Trust, 1960, p. 60.

126. I do not know the source of this quote nor the next one. The quotes were e-mailed to me by a friend.

127. Michael L. Brown, *Whatever Happened to the Power of God*, Destiny Image, 1991,

128. J.I. Packer, *Rediscovering Holiness*, Vine Books, 1992, p. 22.

129. Richard Foster, *Celebration of Discipline*, Harper & Row, 1978, 1988; Henri Nouwen, *The Way of the Heart*, Ballantine Books, 1981.

130. For example, John Wimber, *Power Healing*, Harper & Row, 1987; Francis MacNutt, *The Power to Heal*, Ave Marie Press, 1977; Ken Blue, *Authority to Heal*, InterVarsity Press, 1987.

131. M. Scott Peck, *The Different Drum*, Simon & Schuster, 1987; Larry Crabb, *Connecting*, Word Publishing, 1997.

132. Crabb, op. cit., p. xi.

133. Quoted in Michael Griffiths, *God's Forgetful Pilgrims Recalling the Church to Its Reason for Being*, Eerdmans, 1975, p. 135.

134. Leith Anderson, *Dying for Change*, Bethany House Publishers, 1990, p. 156.

135. Quoted by Don Posterski and Gary Nelson, *Future Faith Churches*, Wood Lake Books, 1997, p. 103.

136. An outstanding book which gives a comprehensive biblical and theological understanding of this is Gordon Fee, *Paul, The Spirit, and the People of God*, Hendrickson Publishers, 1996.

137. George Barna, *Evangelism That Works*, Regal Books, 1995, p. 58.

138. C. Peter Wagner, *Churches That Pray*, Regal Books, 1993, p. 21.

139. See his books, *Churches That Pray*, Ibid., *Warfare Prayer*, Regal Books, 1992, and *Praying With Power*, Regal Books, 1997.

140. Ed Silvoso, 'How to Reach All the Lost in Your City,' in *Ministries Today*, March/April 1997, p. 32.

141. Barna, op. cit., pp. 49–52.

142. Ibid., p. 52–3.

143. Ibid., p. 54.

144. Ibid.

145. Ibid., p. 85.

146. Jimmy Long, op. cit., p. 189–90.

147. Ibid., p. 220.

148. Steve Sjogren, *Conspiracy of Kindness*, Vine Books, 1993.

149. Ibid., p. 49.

150. Ibid., p. 17–18.

151. Clark Pinnock, *Flame of Love: A Theology of the Holy Spirit*, InterVarsity Press, 1996.

152. Op. cit., pp. 211–226.

153. See Roger Helland, *Let the River Flow: Welcoming Renewal Into Your Church*, Bridge-Logos and HarperCollins, 1996, Chapters 11–12.

154. Taken from an interview published in *Ministries Today*, 'What We Can Learn From Argentina's Revival,' March/April 1997, p. 24.

155. Guy Chevreau, *Share the Fire*, Self-published, 1996, p. 40.

156. Roger Helland, op. cit., p. 238.

157. Richard Lovelace, *Dynamics of Spiritual Life*, InterVarsity Press, 1979, p. 381.

158. Win and Charles Arn, *The Master's Plan for Making Disciples*, Church Growth Press, 1982, p. 43.

159. For an excellent treatment of Wesley's patterns for church renewal see Howard A. Snyder, *The Radical Wesley*, Zondervan, 1980.

160. Submitted by Gary Greig with cover letter (garygre@bellatlantic. net) on the New-Wine News Digest (new-wine@grmi.org) November 20, 1997, and forwarded by Richard Riss (RRISS@drew. edu).

161. J. Edwin Orr, *The Eager Feet: Evangelical Awakenings 1790–1830*, Moody Press, 1975, p. 248.

162. David Bryant, *The Hope At Hand*, Baker Books, 1995, p. 105.

163. Charles G. Finney, *Lectures on Revival*, Bethany House Publishers, 1988, pp. 20–21.

164. Teaching notes from Dr Guy Chevreau, at our New Life Vineyard School of Leadership & Renewal, May 1997, citing *The Revival of Religion: Addresses by Scottish Evangelical Leaders, Delivered in Glasgow, 1840*. The Banner of Truth Trust, 1840/1984, Camelot Press, Southampton, p. x.

165. Arthur Wallis, op. cit., p. 59.

166. Brian H. Edwards, *Revival: A People Saturated With God*, Evangelical Press, 1990, p. 128, citing Woolsey, *Duncan Campbell*, Hodder & Stoughton, 1974, p. 133.

167. Earle E. Cairns, *An Endless Line of Splendor*, Tyndale House Publishers, 1986, p. 243.

168. Eifion Evans, *The Welsh Revival of 1904*, Evangelical Press of Wales, 1969, p. 63.

169. J. Edwin Orr, *The Flaming Tongue: The Impact of 20th Century Revivals*, Moody Press, 1973, p. 17.

170. Ibid., p. 20.

171. Richard M. Riss, *A Survey of 20th Century Revival Movements In North America*, Hendrickson Publishers, 1988, p. 50.

172. Frank Bartleman, *Azusa Street: The Roots of Modern-Day Pentecost*, Bridge Publishing, 1980, p. 58–60.

173. Riss, op. cit., p. 47, citing Vinson Synan ed., *Aspects of Pentecostal-Charismatic Origins*, Logos International, 1957, p. 1 and Walter Hollenweger, *The Pentecostals, The Charismatic Movement in the Churches*, Augsburg Publishing House, 1972, pp. xvii-xviii, 29.

174. Stephen Hill, *The Pursuit of Revival*, Creation House, 1997, pp. 73–4.

175. John Kilpatrick, *Feast of Fire*, Self-published, 1995, pp. 72–6.

176. R.E. Davies, *I Will Pour Out My Spirit: A History and Theology of Revivals and Evangelical Awakenings*, Monarch Publications, 1992, p. 217–18.

177. Michael L. Brown, *Whatever Happened to the Power of God*, Destiny Image, 1991, pp. 101–02.

178. Cited from BibleSoft, PC Study Bible, 'Repentance' in *Nelson's Illustrated Bible Dictionary*, Thomas Nelson Publishers, 1986.

179. Brian H. Edwards, op. cit., pp. 119–121.
180. Jonathan Edwards, 'A Narrative of Surprising Conversions,' in *Jonathan Edwards on Revival*, The Banner of Truth Trust, 1984, 1987, p. 21.
181. C. Peter Wagner, *Praying With Power*, Regal Books, 1997, p. 102.
182. John Dawson, *Taking Our Cities For God*, Creation House, 1989; *Healing America's Wounds*, Regal Books, 1994.
183. Wagner, op. cit., pp. 98–99.
184. William Barclay, *The Revelation of John*, Volume 1, Revised Edition, The Westminster Press, 1976, p. 137.
185. Ibid., p. 147–48.
186. Michael L. Brown, *Let No One Deceive You: Confronting the Critics of Revival*, Revival Press, 1997, Chapter 2.
187. Ibid., p. 13, (italics his).
188. Michael L. Brown, *From Holy Laughter to Holy Fire*, Destiny Image, 1996, pp. 42–62.
189. Cited by Edward L. Peet in, *Quotable Quotations*, compiled by Lloyd Cory, Victor Books, 1985, p. 324.
190. Gene Edwards, *The Tale of Three Kings: A Study in Brokenness*, Tyndale House Publishers, 1992, pp. 21–22.
191. 'Some Thoughts Concerning the Revival of Religion in New England' in *The Works of Jonathan Edwards*, The Banner of Truth Trust, 2 Vols. 1992, p. 401.
192. Jim Cymbala, *Fresh Wind Fresh Fire*, Zondervan, 1997, p. 19 (italics mine).
193. Gene Edwards, op. cit., pp. 40–41.
194. Richard M. Riss, *A Survey of 20th Century Revival Movements in North America*, Hendrickson Publishers, 1988, and Richard and Kathryn Riss, *Images of Revival*, Revival Press, 1997. This list is used by permission.